JOURNAL FOR THE STUDY OF THE OLD TESTAMENT
SUPPLEMENT SERIES

27

Editors
David J A Clines
Philip R Davies

Department of Biblical Studies
The University of Sheffield
Sheffield S10 2TN
England

Published by
JSOT Press
Department of Biblical Studies
The University of Sheffield
Sheffield S10 2TN
England

Printed in Great Britain
by Redwood Burn Ltd.,
Trowbridge, Wiltshire.

British Library Cataloguing in Publication Data

Bellinger, W.H.
    Psalmody and prophecy.—(Journal for the
    study of the Old Testament supplement series,
    ISSN 0309-0787; 27)
    1. Bible. O.T. Psalms—Criticism, interpretation,
    etc.   2. Prophets
    I. Title   II. Series
    223′.2   BS1430.2

    ISBN 0-905774-60-4
    ISBN 0-905774-61-2 Pbk

PSALMODY
AND
PROPHECY

W.H. BELLINGER Jr.

Journal for the Study of the Old Testament
Supplement Series 27

CONTENTS

PREFACE

This book is based on a thesis entitled *Psalmody and Prophecy: A Re-examination of the Relationship with Special Reference to Some Recent Cultic and Form Critical Theories* which was submitted to the University of Cambridge for the degree of Ph.D. in 1980. In preparation for this publication, I have undertaken some reorganization and revision of the material and omitted some sections, particularly from the latter part of the work. The Hebrew translations come directly from the text in *BHS*; the Hebrew versification has been followed throughout. It might also be helpful to point out that all Biblical references noted in chapter one are from the Psalms, whether explicitly indicated or not. The phrase 'certainty of a hearing' has been used in relation to laments even though it is rather awkward in English. We have retained the phrase because of its familiarity and its relation to Gunkel's *Gewissheit der Erhörung* and because it clearly expresses the idea that the worshipper is now certain that God hears his prayer.

A project like this owes much to many people; it would be impossible to thank them all. However, my supervisor, Dr R.E. Clements, has been a constant source of encouragement and guidance and I appreciate this greatly. Many family members and friends have aided at various stages of the project and special thanks go to Mary McLerren, typist. This work could not have been done without the support of my wife, Libby, who has spent many hours with its contents. I also wish to thank the editors of the *Journal for the Study of the Old Testament* for their helpful suggestions and their kindness in including the book in their Supplement Series.

The book is dedicated to LDJ, JID and REC—important guides along the way.

W.H. Bellinger, Jr. April, 1982
Southwestern Baptist Theological Seminary
Fort Worth, Texas.

INTRODUCTION

Interpreters of the Old Testament have long recognized a relationship between psalmody and prophecy; however, the definition of that relationship is an old and complex problem. The purpose of this study is to explore various aspects of the relationship in the hope of further defining and explaining it.

We will begin by examining the ways in which other scholars have discussed the relationship between psalmody and prophecy. Initially this issue raised the problem of establishing some kind of chronology for the two kinds of literature in order to trace the direction of influence. Early critical scholarship, exemplified in B. Duhm,[1] understood the prophets to be the great religious innovators in Israel. Thus, any similarity between psalmody and prophecy was the result of the influence of prophecy on the psalmists who composed their spiritual poetry after the period of great prophetic activity before the exile. The psalmists imitated prophetic thoughts and forms and thus the Psalms were of secondary importance.

A shift in this view began with the work of Hermann Gunkel which gives the first notable attention to the question of the relationship between psalmody and prophecy. Gunkel's article on the Psalms in the first edition of *RGG* furnishes a good beginning point.[2] The basic argument in that article has to do with the literary types found in the Psalter and proposes that the sources for Psalm study must also include those Psalms in the Old Testament which are not in the Psalter as well as extra-biblical psalms. In the course of Gunkel's description of the literary types found in the Psalms, he notes that the same types are found in the prophetic books. The prophets used religious lyric poetry to make an impression on the people and as a means of expressing their feelings. Gunkel notes several examples of the occurrence of the same forms in the Psalms and the Prophets. For example the first two chapters of Joel are a liturgy on a disastrous locust plague imploring God to have mercy on his people. Various ritual acts accompanied this liturgy just as they did the Psalms. Gunkel also pointed out the oracular element in the

Psalms, especially the Royal Psalms; the oracle is one of the primary prophetic speech-forms. This last point is of particular significance for our study. Since Gunkel took the view that the Psalms had their origin in the cult but came to break free of that liturgical religion and became spiritual poems, it is understandable that he saw the chronological influence to be primarily but not exclusively from prophet to psalmist. However, for the purposes of this study, it is very important to note that Gunkel recognized the same literary forms and often the same content in much of psalmody and prophecy.

The most important work by Gunkel on the topic at hand is found in his *Einleitung in die Psalmen*.[3] Here he carries the discussion further by describing the prophets' considerable influence on the Psalms. He sees this influence first of all in the eschatology of the Psalter. Gunkel's reconstruction of that eschatology includes several elements. First is the restoration of the city of Zion and the people Israel. They are to be liberated with Yahweh enthroned on Zion. The picture is carried further by saying that the heathen enemies are to be caught in the pits which they themselves have made. They will receive the fate prepared for another; this is divine retribution upon their unrighteousness. Then there are also the natural disasters of the end-time. This is especially seen in the Zion Songs as Yahweh comes to set up a new world order. Also in these psalms we find Yahweh's battle with the tumultuous sea which Gunkel compares with Yahweh's victory over the peoples threatening Israel in the Prophets. Yahweh protects Zion as he rules over the unrighteous in anger. Then, of course, comes Yahweh's worldwide rule; he rules as king from Zion, the delight of the world. Though seen more in the later prophets than in the Psalms, there is also the hope of extending Israel's rule. Finally as this brings great rejoicing on earth, it also brings great rejoicing in heaven. Even the other gods praise Yahweh. Gunkel took the view that the psalmists borrowed much of this eschatological picture from the prophets and it became very important in Israel's festivals. He dated most of the psalms with prophetic elements in the post-exilic period, coming after Deutero-Isaiah. There is a great deal of similarity of content here, even to the point of using the same terminology in these pictures, but the psalmists do not use all the prophetic eschatology; so there are also some distinctions.

Gunkel notes that as there is a similarity in eschatological content there is also a similarity in the forms used to express this content in the Psalter and the prophetic books; form and content generally go together. The forms which Gunkel mentions include the hymn with its jubilation over God's great future action, such as the Zion Songs and the Enthronement Songs. The prophetic eschatological hope is also seen in the sections of trust and certainty of a hearing in the individual community laments. Especially in the latter, as Israel is in the midst of trouble and sinks further into a crisis like the Babylonian exile, her hopes for the future are put off but also become very important as a means of victory over the heathen enemies. Gunkel also finds eschatology in the Wisdom Psalms in the sayings of blessing and cursing.

Gunkel notes further prophetic elements in the Psalter in forms not specifically related to eschatology. This is often in the mixed types and liturgies found in the Psalter. The oracle has been borrowed from the Prophets and used in the liturgy and prophetic calls for righteousness are reflected in similar exhortations in laments in the Psalter. Warnings including threat and promise are in both psalmody and prophecy and the prophetic polemic against the overestimation of sacrifice is also reflected in the Psalms at times. In addition, the scoffing at foreign gods which is often seen in Deutero-Isaiah is found in the Psalter. The prophetic influence is also to be seen in the moral nature of the Torah Liturgies.

While Gunkel is certainly mistaken in seeing much of the relationship between psalmody and prophecy in terms of eschatology, this in no way questions the similarity he saw between the two kinds of literature. He was also bound by much of the late dating of the Psalms and this led him to see most of the borrowing to be from prophet to psalmist. Nonetheless Gunkel has clearly defined a number of important prophetic elements in the Psalter. It is his methodology which is most significant; similarity of literary forms and content in those forms is the beginning point. Upon this basis, we may begin to speak of prophetic elements in the Psalms.

The next major step in investigating the relationship between the Psalms and prophecy was taken by the Norwegian scholar Sigmund Mowinckel. In his *Psalmenstudien* III, it is clear that he had heard Gunkel saying that psalmody and prophecy are related but he took a different approach.[4] Gunkel had understood many psalms to originate in the cult but said they were freed from that cultic setting later. Mowinckel, however, finds both the origin and use of most psalms in the cult and so places what he classifies as prophetic psalms firmly in the cult.[5] For Mowinckel the prophetic word is an important component of the cult in the inspired pronouncement of God's answer to the worshippers. So he concentrates on and expands Gunkel's suggestion concerning the oracular element within the Psalms.

Mowinckel spends a great deal of time surveying his theory of the various cult functionaries, their origins, development, and distinctions. He seeks to substantiate the existence of cult prophets. However, he does not necessarily equate the canonical prophets with cult prophets. Historically, the seer and priest were the same person, the keeper of the sanctuary. Moses and Samuel are examples of this type of cultic functionary. Somewhere along the way in Israel, however, these two functions came to be separated. The seer moved more toward the prophetic function and the priest became a mediator of Yahweh's revelation in the cult; he pronounced the priestly oracle. This often came with the casting of lots with the Urim and Thummim. The נביא, prophet, is of Canaanite origin and not as old as the seer. Mowinckel finds this prophetic origin not to be priestly; it is separate. And yet the נביאים do function in relation to the sanctuaries. They are temple prophets, part of an institution, an organization of temple functionaries which owes much to the seer and the cult. They were ecstatic, visionary, and came to be bearers of revelation in many ways. They were freely inspired and functioned in the cult. These people were also related to the music of the cult as ecstasy might imply, and in the end the institutional cult prophet faded into the musical background of the cult. Mowinckel also discusses the various ways of determining the cult oracle and finds no basic distinction between the prophetic and priestly methods.

He then seeks to relate this material to the biblical psalms. Oracles are often found in psalms, many of them cult-liturgical compositions of many voices. Mowinckel considers these to be prophetic psalms. He discusses these various psalms according to their cultic settings: the annual New Year Festival, the occasional worship of the community, worship occasions associated with the king and finally private cultic acts. His attention focuses upon the oracular element in the psalms, spoken in a prophetic style. The inspired cult prophet speaks Yahweh's word to the people, whether king or nation or individual. These oracles are often in response to laments and prayers for help, though the elements of blessing and warning in the context of worship are also present. So Mowinckel also sees the prophetic element in the Psalter in terms of form and content but this leads him to posit the existence of cult prophets. He understands their work to be found primarily in the oracles in the Psalms.

It is also very important that Mowinckel gives two examples of cult prophecy which have been noted and expanded by later authors. The first is the prophecy of Habakkuk. He calls Habakkuk a cult prophet and psalm poet, and takes the first two chapters of the prophetic book to be a psalm, a lament and prayer liturgy. Habakkuk 3 is a cultic psalm, a trust psalm based on Yahweh's past great works. The second example is the book of Joel, which mixes the psalm style and the prophetic style.

Thus Mowinckel sees a clear relationship between psalmody and prophecy; he affirms the similarity in form and content in both kinds of literature with his consideration of the place of the oracle in the Psalms and of the psalmic style in Habakkuk and Joel.[6] This greatly influences his case for the existence of cult prophets.[7] In large measure because of Mowinckel's work it is now generally agreed that the Psalms have chronological priority and consequently much of the influence must originate there.[8] In addition, with the work of Gunkel and Mowinckel the issue has moved further in dealing with the similarities and distinctions between psalmody and prophecy and how we may account for these.

It is clearly not the case that Mowinckel was the first to conceive of cult prophets in Israel. Smith[9] and Hölscher[10] were both precursors in this. However, it was Mowinckel who supported the argument sufficiently and saw its consequences. He is the initiator of the emphasis and interest shown in cult prophecy in recent Old Testament scholarship, and since his work, cult prophecy has been the most popular way of accounting for the similarities between the Psalms and the prophetic literature. The prophetic element in the Psalter comes from prophets among the cultic personnel, cult prophets. The situation is more complicated with the canonical prophets, but the psalmic element there has in some cases been accounted for by the assertion that the prophet was influenced by the tradition of cult prophets.

A number of other scholars have investigated this problem and several have understood the נביאים to be related to the cult in some way,[11] but probably the next major step in the study of the problem was a monograph on the cult prophet by Aubrey Johnson.[12] He also understands the early נביאים to be closely associated with the formal worship of Yahweh in the sanctuary; they are cultic specialists. That cult prophets were not the only kind of prophet in Israel is seen from the evidence contained in the prophetic books. Here the canonical prophets engage in much polemic against the abuse of the office of (cult) prophet and the giving of false oracles. This seems to indicate that there was a regular traffic of oracles in this period in Israel as in other parts of the world, and the cult prophet would have been the source of many of these. He was a specialist in prayer, an intercessor who spoke the prayer and the oracle, God's response to the prayer. Thus, he served a dual role as cultic mediator between God and man and as such played a vital role among the cult personnel in the Jerusalem temple. These prophets were officially a part of the temple cult as were the priests with whom they are often coupled in the Old Testament. The status of the cult prophets was not a subordinate one but was at least as high as that of the priests. Following Mowinckel, Johnson uses his arguments for the existence of cult prophets to account for the prophetic elements in the Psalms. In his earlier article, he asserts that prayers as well as the oracular elements in psalms may come from cult prophets.

In his latest volume, Johnson expands this by discussing the psalms in which he finds cult prophets to have been active in intercession and the proclamation of the divine response to prayer.[13] His interesting treatment is in three parts: the responsibility of the cult prophet for the life of society as seen in regular worship, then as seen in times of national crisis, and the cult prophet's responsibility for the life of the individual in times of personal crisis. Johnson works with a similar methodology to that used by Mowinckel though he uses his own definition of the task of cult prophets as articulated in his earlier volume. He is very much concerned with the form and content of texts and understands the psalms he deals with as functioning in areas which relate to cult prophecy. He understands the cult prophet to have had a dual role of offering intercession and conveying the divine response to such prayer. Thus he perceives their function to be primarily educational and regards entire psalms as the work of cult prophets who used them to exhort the people to the life of faith. Within such a task, the prophet would preserve and transmit to the people the historical traditions of the faith, such as the Davidic covenant, seeking to encourage them in righteousness. This type of 'up-building' function was carried out in community crises such as war and particularly in crises concerning the king whose well-being the prophet protected. The psalms from cult prophets were used as models to remind the people that Yahweh protects the faithful. So Johnson in no way limits prophetic elements in the Psalms to oracular sections. He does begin with that phenomenon but then expands it to include whole prayers which can relate to the cult prophetic function, often that of encouraging the people to the life of faith and righteousness. This means that Johnson uses the notion of the function of a text to help in determining whether it can be considered prophetic, but relates that function closely to his own particular understanding of cult prophets and their role in ancient Israel. Such a view broadens the understanding of prophetic elements in the Psalms significantly and may raise the question of where we should stop. If we follow Johnson's lead at this point, much of the Psalter could be labeled 'prophetic' and should be related to cult prophets. However, this generally well-argued volume is particularly important in that it raises again a question which is central to our concerns: what constitutes a prophetic element in the Psalms?

The cult prophet theory was taken even further in 1945 by a young Swedish scholar, A. Haldar.[14] Haldar's work compares the cult prophet phenomenon in the various Semitic religions. In Israel the נביא is an ecstatic cult functionary, and this phenomenon is no different from that found in the nations surrounding Israel. Haldar also takes the view that the canonical prophets are part of the cult prophet phenomenon; all prophets are on the same level. These prophets functioned in groups usually with a leader, sometimes the king, at the local sanctuaries and the various cultic festivals, reciting rituals and oracles. By way of divination, they had special knowledge of God and communicated this word from Yahweh in the cult. This is certainly an extreme statement of the cult prophet theory and fails to take adequate note of the distinctiveness of Israel's religion when comparing it with those of neighbouring peoples.

There have been a number of other studies relevant to the topic at hand, most of which seek to relate the נביאים to the cult in some way[15] or to see them as a part of the official religious establishment in Israel.[16] The list of scholars supporting the existence of cult prophets in ancient Israel would be too long to reproduce here.[17]

Scholars such as E. Würthwein and H. Graf Reventlow have sought strongly to support the form-critical part of the argument for cult prophets. Würthwein does this by finding the origin of the prophetic *Gerichtsrede* in the cult.[18] This speech form must have a distinctive setting because it is used so frequently and in a constant form. The setting Würthwein discovers is the cultic accusation and judgment from Yahweh pronounced by cultic personnel, most likely cult prophets. In another study, Würthwein also finds a cultic setting for the prophetic sayings opposing the cult.[19] This is in the divine reply given to prayer which was pronounced by the cult prophet. The canonical prophets take the positive reply to prayer and make it into a negative one in order to announce judgment against particular cultic acts. Reventlow works with a similar understanding of speech forms—a fixed form indicating an institutional setting.[20] He begins by examining the prophetic message formula and finds its origin in the giving of the law in the covenant feast. So he sees the prophetic office as firmly based in the cult and as mediating the law. These scholars do not identify the canonical prophets with these cultic officials in every case but still see prophecy in ancient Israel as basically an institution closely related to the cult.[21]

Much has been written in support of the existence of cult prophecy in Israel and this has remained the most common basis for relating psalmody and prophecy.[22] Today it is virtually the orthodox position to understand cult prophecy as the explanation of prophetic elements in the Psalms. Even so, there have been some notable exceptions to this rule.

The institutional approach to prophecy exemplified by Würthwein and Reventlow has been challenged by several scholars.[23] Hesse in particular opposes Würthwein's view that the prophetic *Gerichtsrede* had its setting in the cult. The judgment he finds in the cultic literature of the Psalms is essentially different from that in the canonical prophets.[24]

A more basic objection is that presented by G. Quell,[25] who sees the existence of cult prophets as a hypothesis without a historically confirmed basis. It is based on analogy in the interpretation of some psalms and it would need to be proved in a historical, rather than a form-critical, way that the liturgist in the psalms should be called a cult prophet before the hypothesis could be accepted. This is the case primarily because prophetic words can easily be imitated in liturgy rather than actually coming from a prophet. The prophetic words can be taken from their original setting and put into an institutional one in order to proclaim their message in that different setting. This same issue is raised by de Vaux.[26] He also takes the view that it cannot be proved that prophets were attached to the Jerusalem temple or part of its clergy, though prophets and priests did both instruct in religion and may both have had some connections with the cult and temple. However, this does not mean that they were a part of the staff there.

Though he is not opposed to the cult prophet theory in its totality, H.H. Rowley also raises several questions concerning it.[27] He makes an important and convincing case for the fact that one cannot divide the prophets in Israel into clear-cut, well-defined classes. There were evidently many varieties of prophet. Neither is there any simple pattern which can be imposed on early prophecy. Early נביאים could function at sanctuaries or at home or at the court or in the wayside. Some prophets may have had an official standing at the temple and have been consulted on special cultic days, but this does not mean that all prophets fall into this category.[28] Further, the fact that a prophet functioned in the precincts of a shrine does not mean that he was performing an official activity.[29] Rowley points out that if the term is to have any meaning a cult prophet must be one with a defined part in the official services of the temple or shrine and not just a person who speaks to groups of people in the precincts of the sanctuary. He also points out elsewhere that it is very difficult to define precisely the functions of any cult prophets or their relationship with other prophets.[30] Finally, Rowley raises the same objection as Quell but in relation to the prophets. That is, it is entirely possible that the canonical prophets could have imitated liturgical forms for their own purposes. The fact that they use such forms does not necessarily mean that they are cultic functionaries.[31]

One of the latest works on this topic is that by J. Jeremias.[32] He understands the existence of cult prophets to be fairly certain in the mid- to late monarchical period in Israel. The early prophets were connected with the sanctuaries and questions were brought to them on feast days, although it is hard to define clearly their relationship to the cult. Information on cultic prophets at the Jerusalem temple is, however, more definite. They gave Yahweh's word in the oracle and interceded for the people there. If the canonical prophets could be included in cult prophecy, we should be able to get a clearer view of their message, and some scholars have taken this path. However, one of the difficulties with this position is that, if the canonical prophets who pronounced doom were cult prophets, then the cult prophets of the late pre-exilic period in Israel must also have announced doom. So we have the problem of relating cult prophecy to the announcement of judgment. The two are not necessarily mutually exclusive. Jeremias then examines the prophecies of Nahum and Habakkuk from this point of view to determine whether they are to be regarded as cultic prophets. This topic will be mentioned later. Jeremias goes on to examine traces of cult prophecy in the Psalter. He finds that there does appear to be some kind of judgment proclaimed there. It is not a judgment against foreign nations or against the nation of Israel; it is rather against the guilty in Israel. The cult prophets seek to purify Israel of any evil so that Yahweh can intervene to save his people. They use both cultic and prophetic speech-forms as well as wisdom concepts and language. The lament liturgy is one of the genuine cult-prophetic forms in which the prophets inquire of Yahweh by seeking an oracle. They may seek to find the cause of some evil or intercede for someone. This was an official cultic function recognized by the priests and perhaps performed during the ceremony by making confession of the guilt of the people in accompaniment with fasts during times of crisis. This may be where the cult-prophetic liturgies were set—on occasional feasting days with lament and petition.

Jeremias continues by rejecting Würthwein's view that the prophetic *Gerichtsrede*, or the prophetic words against the cult, originated in the cult with the cult prophets. The cult prophet seeks Israel's salvation in crises and the judgment he announces is to that end; he still accepts the covenant and election traditions. The prophets of doom are compelled by Yahweh to prophesy. They are not involved in a ceremony, nor do they belong to any office. Judgment on all Israel is at the centre of their message since they see the nation threatened with a complete end. Thus, the cult prophets and prophets of woe are a real contrast of type. Cultic prophets were probably in groups with a leader and generally remained at the temple. They probably dealt with sacrificial signs and dreams in the temple and were closely related to king, priest and temple. The canonical prophets of woe were not of this institutional type. They opposed the cult prophets not in principle but because they abused their function. Cult prophecy was closely bound to its original setting, but prophecy of woe was preserved and reinterpreted many times and the worth of its message came to be recognized.

This treatment of the topic at hand is quite interesting but does not appear to move us further in defining the relationship between psalmody and prophecy. The various categories of judgment and prophecy are difficult and complex and ultimately not helpful; they rather confuse the issue. Such an institutional approach to the study of prophecy encounters many difficulties.

With the exception of Aubrey Johnson's new volume, there seems to have been little of significance written on the subject of this investigation since the publication of Jeremias' book in 1970. Thus it appears to be an appropriate time to look at the matter again. The present situation is that some sort of relationship between psalmody and prophecy is widely recognized but needs to be defined more precisely.

A number of prophetic elements in the Psalter have already been discussed. These include blessings, cursing, hymnic anticipations of God's victory, intercession, and warnings and exhortations concerning loyalty to Yahweh and his ethical norms. However, the primary prophetic element which has been identified in the Psalter is the oracle. In it Yahweh's word is made known to his people.

In addition it has become clear that the canonical prophets were not simply opposed to the cult. Beyond this, there are difficulties in analysing the various categories of prophecy because there was such a great variety within prophecy in Israel and individual prophets did not belong to only one tradition of prophetic activity. Thus, it is best not to be side-tracked into seeking to categorize prophets and their messages. It appears rather that we can better attempt to deal with on the one hand the early, or pre-classical, prophets and on the other the classical or canonical prophets.[33] It has already been seen that there is some evidence connecting early prophets in Israel with sanctuaries. However, early prophecy is still quite obscure and it would be a mistake to make too much of the limited evidence available. There is substance to some of the criticism of the cult prophet theory mentioned above. We must therefore remain somewhat sceptical about cultic prophets even in this sphere, and it is certainly difficult to define their work with any kind of precision. It is also very difficult to relate Israel's early prophets to the later canonical prophets, since there is little material in the Old Testament to help with this task.

The problem of relating the canonical prophets to the cult centres on a fundamental methodological question, that of the relationship between form and setting. Prophets certainly used forms that were originally cultic. Does this mean that they were cultic prophets? It is important that this term be defined first of all. In order for it to have a significant meaning, it must indicate that the prophet was a member of a sanctuary or temple staff regularly and that he had a definite place in the cult—the organized, official worship of Israel in that place. Does the fact that the canonical prophets use cultic speech-forms mean that they are cult prophets in this sense? Were such speech-forms always tied to their original setting? Further, and more central to our concerns, does the fact that oracular forms are found in the Psalms indicate that cult prophets are among the cult personnel and responsible for these elements in the Psalter? Is the cult prophet theory the means of explaining the relationship between psalmody and prophecy? Since Mowinckel, as we have seen, this has been the predominant way of dealing with the question. It is understandable how this came to be the prevailing view, since Mowinckel was clearly influenced by Gunkel's form-critical studies and his assertion that major speech-forms have a setting somewhere in Israel's social and religious life. Upon finding material in the Psalms which is like that of the Prophets, he surmised that this also has a prophetic origin; it comes from cult prophets. But the question is whether forms primary to the Prophets were always bound to the prophet. This is central to the argument for cult prophecy, and this question of the relationship between form and setting and its implications are at the centre of the problems we are investigating.

Our study will centre upon prophetic elements in the Psalms, some of which have been identified, in the hope of further defining and explaining these elements. The delineation of the form and content of texts will be essential to our discussion of psalms since this task is prerequisite to drawing any conclusions concerning the texts' relationship to prophecy. This, of course, builds particularly on the method and work of Gunkel described above and is employed here because it makes clear that the biblical texts are the primary source for conclusions.

It is also relevant to raise again the question of the function of the material as a basic element in the treatment. A word needs to be said about the term 'function'. Rather than concentrating exclusively on a specific aspect of the function of texts,[34] our investigation attempts to look at the question of function in the Psalms in a much broader perspective. What is the intention and purpose to which the material is directed? What is it doing and trying to get its hearers or readers to do? This makes the context of the forms used very important. For what purpose is the form used, and what is its function and the best setting for this? Prophecy is generally related to a particular historical setting while psalmody is usually understood to function in worship and so to be timeless, repeatable and not tied to a particular historical setting.[35] Determining the validity of this distinction, and its relevance to our task, will be part of the present inquiry.

We will concentrate on selected texts among the lament psalms, one of the major categories in the discussion of prophetic elements in the Psalter.[36] These studies of texts focusing on form, content and function will be used to draw conclusions concerning the definition of prophetic elements in the Psalter and the relationship between psalmody and prophecy.

Chapter One

PRELIMINARY CONSIDERATIONS
IN THE STUDY OF THE PSALMS OF LAMENTATION

It will be helpful at this point to outline very briefly the various parts of the lament. These psalms do not all exhibit a fixed structural outline but most of the elements which are set out below usually occur and frequently in the order given.[1] This brief discussion will give the essential context of the texts which are then discussed in more detail in the two following chapters. It also will continue the whole process of the comparison of texts which is so crucial to psalm study and to this investigation.

I *Invocation* The first section of the lament psalm is the address or invocation of the divine name. This is at the beginning of the psalm as might be expected since the lament is usually a prayer to God.[2] The simplest expression of the invocation can be seen in Ps 3:2 with the first word of the psalm being a vocative יהוה. In some places there is added a description of God as the helper and protector of the worshipper(s) (Pss. 4.2; 5.3; 80.2).[3] There is also often connected with the invocation an introductory plea for hearing and answering (5.2; 59.2,3; 83.2).[4] The invocation and related material can anticipate much of the remainder of the psalm (Pss. 42-43; 51).[5]

II *Lament* The next section in the lamentation psalm is the lament proper. The character of the psalm as a lamentation comes from the occasion behind this section, for herein is described the distress which brings about the prayer. In an unrestrained way, the worshipper, or group of worshippers, sketches for Yahweh a picture of his plight of oppression and torment and of his inner sorrow and despair.[6] The most frequent theme of the lament proper is that of complaints regarding enemies of the lamenter or the nation (10.2-11; 57.5; 140.4; 12.3,5; 58.4-6). The threat of death is also a part of the crisis at hand (55.5; 88.4-19). In other places, the worshipper(s) confesses his sin and laments its consequences (51.13). Similarly a significant part of the crisis described in this section is related to God's anger or the feeling that God is absent (Pss. 6; 42-43; 90.7-10). In the community laments, the crisis is often described in terms of military defeat (44.10ff.; 74.4-11).[7]

III *Petition* The petition is the part of the lament which reveals the purpose of the psalm. The purpose of the prayer is to request something from God and that is precisely what this section does.[8] The primary petition is for Yahweh to answer the worshipper(s) (13.4; 86.6; 142.7). He desires deliverance from the crisis at hand (3.8; 28.3; 9.20; 17.7; 85.5-8; 126.4,5) and seeks Yahweh's protection. A large number of the petitions concern the enemies of the petitioner or the nation (7.10; 140.10f.; 28.4; 58.7-10; 83.10-19).[9] There is also the petition that Yahweh may teach the worshipper the divine path (27.11; 143.10) and keep him from sin (141.3f.). The desire for deliverance and a return to the prosperity and joy of the presence of God are clearly enunciated in these texts (90.13-17).

IV *Motivation(s)* The motivations attempt to give reasons for Yahweh to answer the prayer. Since the aim of the prayer is to stir Yahweh to act on behalf of the worshipper or nation, these motivations are quite important. A significant amount of space is given to them in the psalms though not usually in a separate section. One of the most frequent reasons given for answering the prayer is the trust of the worshipper(s) (25.5; 69.7ff.).[10] God is also urged to answer the prayer for the sake of his honour. His past deeds of kindness are brought to mind to support this motivation (102.26ff.; 44.2-9; 80.9-12). The worshipper's, or nation's, penitence may also be used as a motivation for the answer of prayer (25.11; 79.8,9). The distress itself is also used in this way (5.9; 27.12; 31.10; 88.4). This is all in support of the aim of the psalm, to persuade God to act on behalf of the lamenter or nation in the midst of a crisis.

V *Certainty of a Hearing* This element of the lament psalm expresses the certainty that the prayer is now heard. The worshipper's, or community's, wavering and seeking of certainty is now a thing of the past; there is no longer the need for petition and motivation because an answer is now certain. This material uses what is in the petitions but in sure expectation of a favourable divine response.[11] The sudden change of mood in the psalm from lament, sorrow and petition to joy and certainty is what first calls attention to this phenomenon. Its simplest manifestation is the statement that the prayer is heard (6.10; 28.6). Then there is also the expression of the certainty of Yahweh's deliverance (55.18-20,23; 27.13; 28.7; 12.6f.). Since the enemies are so prominent in the petitions, it is only natural

that there are several expressions of the certainty of their downfall
(3.8; 6.11; 60.14); the petitions are answered.

VI *Vow* The vow often closes the psalm and is basically a promise to
God by the worshipper(s), usually a promise of praise and thanksgiving.[12] On some occasions, the vow itself leads to praise which
ends the psalm and actually fulfils the vow. In places the vow is to
offer sacrifices with shouts (27.6; 54.8). The more frequent vows,
however, are for praise and thanksgiving (7.18; 22.23ff.; 26.12;
79.13). The prayer is answered and thanksgiving expressed.

Various attempts have been made to classify the lament psalms, and
especially the individual laments, into more specific categories such
as prayers of the falsely accused[13] or prayers of sick persons.[14]
However, the broader categories of individual and community lament
are retained here for methodological and substantive reasons. Such
categories give more space for comparison and a broader base for the
discussion. The laments display a similar basic form and content and
thus should be categorized together; their dominant similarities
allow them to be analyzed into a literary class. It is also the case that
the more detailed cult-functional classifications cannot be applied to
all of the psalms under discussion. While they no doubt are applicable
to some psalms, none of the smaller categories fit all of the psalms.
Thus the category 'lament psalm' has been retained in this investigation.
Various kinds of individual and community laments and their cultic
settings will be considered in the following chapters.

Before this is done, however, several comments need to be made
concerning the nature of the language of the laments. This is an
important consideration because it is the language that texts exhibit
which forms the basis for classifying them; it is also the primary
evidence in seeking to determine the occasions of the laments as well
as identifying the enemies and the worshippers. So a description of
the nature of the language is an important prerequisite to their
detailed study.

Most interpreters of the psalms note the general character of their
language.[15] Gunkel particularly emphasizes this in the *Einleitung*.
In discussing the nature of the distress described in the individual
lament, he says it is very difficult and often impossible to determine
the situation presupposed from the images used. There are few
tangible helps in the psalms towards identifying the outward circumstances of the worshipper.[16] This is at the base of the problem of

classifying the psalms in any detailed way. Often the language of lament psalms is vague and of a universal character. This characteristic allows a psalm to have a wide appeal but it also causes commentators great difficulty in establishing its particular cultic setting with any kind of specificity. Such is true of the individual laments and of the community laments, though in the latter there are some clear descriptions of situations including military defeats. However, even these descriptions are so formulaic as to make any delineation of the specific historical situation very difficult.

The general nature of the psalmodic language has been explained in various ways.[17] It does not seem appropriate to describe the psalms as merely cultic formulas, but it certainly appears to be true that they were used in the cult. Thus they were probably written, or at least preserved, in a form suitable for use by different people in many similar situations. Here is part of the reason for their vagueness, as Mowinckel points out.[18] Gunkel points to the desire to emphasize the spiritual as part of the explanation.[19] The use of very general language is also well attested in the psalm literature from nations surrounding Israel.[20] But there is another consideration in this connection which has not been given the full attention it deserves. A psalm written for an individual's use could have been modified through the years to make it more applicable to the community in a changed situation.[21] It is possible that many psalms were composed for certain situations and then generalized in order to broaden their usability to include additional contexts; in this way they became reusable. It is at least the case that the influence of the use of the psalms through the centuries must be given consideration when discussing their language and how it developed. It may well have been changed to fit the needs of the community and the purposes of its worship in varying situations. This development must be considered as another way of explaining the general nature of the language of the lament psalms.

There is another question in attempting to characterize the language of the lament psalms which goes further in trying to ascertain whether the language is to be taken literally, mythologically or metaphorically. Those who understand the laments to come from specific situations in the lives of the worshipper or nation understand the words of these psalms in a literal way. Thus the language of Ps. 38 is understood clearly to describe the circumstances of a sick person.[22] A mythological interpretation of the language of the laments would entail understanding the lament section describing the sojourn in the underworld in mythological terms. Death described in these sections of the laments is a threatening power, which is part of a mythical world view. There are clearly parallel myths of death as a power in nations surrounding Israel, especially Ugarit, and these are seen as important in creation and the ordering of life. Perhaps this mythical environment has left its mark on the laments.[23] Others have supported a figurative interpretation of the language of these psalms.[24] There are many metaphors in them such as the descriptions of the enemies as wild animals or hunters but this understanding of the psalmic language goes further in seeing texts such as Ps. 6, for example, as not referring literally to a sick person but simply as a vivid way of describing dire distress.

It is generally agreed that there is a literal component to the language in these texts, particularly when referring to actual cultic events or historical moments such as the fall of Jerusalem. This element is usually combined with either a mythological or metaphorical meaning reflected in the texts. Since Mowinckel much less attention has been given to the metaphorical approach, which is unfortunate because the boundary between metaphor and myth is not always clear-cut.[25] Metaphor can lead to myth and so myth may reflect a metaphorical background. Further, a watered-down version of myth can in many cases more properly be understood as metaphor. The mythological understanding of the language can be lost or at least recede into the background. Also, it seems accurate to say that in its present state, much of the language of the laments is figurative in nature. This is one of the reasons why the language causes such problems. It is very difficult to be precise about the meanings and background of words with such a highly figurative and metaphorical content, which of course in no way makes any less real the experiences this language reflects. Actual, vivid and important experiences can be expressed figuratively. So the question of the nature of the language in these laments is a complex one. Perhaps various levels of understanding are present. Here is a possibility which warrants further study in psalm research.

It is essential that the problem of the nature of the language be considered before an interpreter proceeds to the detailed cult-functional analysis of psalm texts. His understanding of the language will affect his results. Thus he needs to examine the way he approaches the language and why. The general nature of the language noted above is also significant. A commentator should not expect too much from the psalm text he is interpreting. He can give various possibilities for what is behind the psalm but must often leave open any conclusion because of the vague nature of the language involved. And there is also the possibility that these texts were written with such language in order to allow and even encourage ✓ their interpretation on various levels.

These two aspects of the description of the nature of the language of the psalms of lamentation—its general character and whether it is literal, mythological or metaphorical language—are essential considerations in the study of laments. This is also true of the *Gattungen* analysis in the earlier part of this chapter. That analysis, along with the consideration of the nature of the language of these psalms, gives the context of the psalms treated in detail in the next two chapters.

Excursus I

THE ROYAL INTERPRETATION OF LAMENT PSALMS

There is another way of classifying lament psalms, which needs further consideration. This classification relates to the old question of the identity of the 'I' of these psalms. Much of the concern about this issue was reflected in an extensive article by Rudolf Smend in 1888.[1] Prior to this time, many scholars dated the psalms quite late and related them to the conflicts in Judaism in the post-exilic age. Smend mounted a strong challenge to this view in advocating the position that the 'I' found in many psalms might well be a personification of the community of Israel. Though Smend's position is important in the history of Psalm study, it has been successfully refuted by Emil Balla in *Das Ich der Psalmen*,[2] which gives the definitive explication of the 'I' of the Psalms. Though many of the insights for this almost certainly originated with Gunkel, Balla clearly sets out the case for true individual psalms in the Psalter. This appears to be the most appealing view at present and is not without significance, for it may well be that these psalms are a primary link between the individual and the national religion in Israel. However, this issue continues to be a matter of concern in Psalm study and relates to the royal interpretation of some lament psalms which was taken up by Mowinckel in his later work on the Psalms.[3]

However, mention must first be made of Harris Birkeland, a pupil of Mowinckel, whose work persuaded his teacher to accept the royal interpretation. Birkeland's work is primarily on the enemies in the Psalms.[4] Beginning with those psalms in which the enemies are most likely national enemies and then moving to the other psalms that describe enemies, he comes to the conclusion that throughout the Psalter the enemies are to be understood as national enemies of Israel. This conclusion leads to the view that the individual psalms concerned were spoken by someone representing the people—the king or some other national leader. Birkeland's position is rather restrictive and appears methodologically unsound in positing that all the enemies must be national enemies if some can be shown to be. He does attempt to account for this in part by asserting that the psalms were composed according to patterns, but his position takes this theory too far.[5] Birkeland indicates that a situation, pattern and 'author' are necessary to bring about a psalm but he does not give enough attention to the situation and 'author' in the psalms. The pattern seems to override them and level all the relevant psalms to the same basic profile. Birkeland sees clearly the 'conventional monotony' in the descriptions of the enemies but does not come to grips with the 'confusing variety' which is also present.[6] It is quite possible that some of the enemies in the individual laments are national enemies but that is far from affirming Birkeland's arguments.

Mowinckel takes up this view, but not without modification.[7] His standpoint represents a change in his position concerning these laments.[8] Mowinckel agrees that some of the laments in the 'I-form' are royal psalms and that the enemies concerned are national ones.[9] He understands these 'national psalms of lamentation in the I-form' to be the earlier form of the lament reflecting the earlier collective way of thinking in Israel. The king represents the corporate entity, his people, before Yahweh in situations of national distress and seeks divine help. The psalms are spoken from the point of view of the king and so are primarily interested in the king rather than the people he represents. Thus, the texts speak of the problems he would have with political as well as military enemies and use the terms of his intimate relationship with Yahweh which go beyond that described for other individuals. Mowinckel points to the alternation between 'I' and 'we' in the psalm, the martial terms used and the personification of Israel as oppressed by the nations to support his position. He also notes Babylonian and Assyrian parallels. This royal dimension is not immediately manifest in the psalms under consideration because of a process which has come to be called 'democratizing' whereby original royal psalms are modified enough to allow their use by others later in Israel's worship. Though it is true that the king played an important part in Israel's cult, a fact which Mowinckel uses to great advantage, his interpretation is much too subjective to overcome the arguments for true individual laments given primarily by Balla. It also needs to be said that all the individual laments have a similar form and content. Thus why should it be posited that they come from two strikingly different situations? While Mowinckel's position on this question is certainly more reasonable and cautious than some of the proponents of the royal interpretation of these psalms, it still seems appropriate to consider the psalms relevant to this discussion as individual laments.

The royal interpretation of the laments has recently been supported by John Eaton.[10] While it may be conceded that Eaton has made a contribution in the attempt to locate the origin of some of the terminology in these psalms, his general arguments for the royal interpretation seem to carry little weight. It may be helpful to discuss these.[11]

1. לדוד *in many of the psalm titles shows that royal psalmody has an important place in the Psalter.* This may be countered by the explanation that לדוד indicates that psalms with this in the superscription are a part of the official liturgical collection of the temple and carry royal approval rather than indicating that they are royal psalmody in the way Eaton intends that

label. Eaton also, with no serious comment, delineates as royal a number of psalms without לדוד in the title.

2.   *The tradition of David as psalmist and of psalmody arising from the king* is really no testimony against a non-royal interpretation of these psalms. Their presence in the official collection, of which the king was patron, does not make them 'Royal Psalms'.

3.   *The king was important in Israelite religion*. This might support the view that a royal interpretation of these psalms would fit Israel's religion but it does not substantiate the view that these texts are royal psalms.

4.   *Since the king's situation is a 'known' context of some psalms and it is difficult to determine the situations of other psalms, this 'known' setting should be applied more widely*. This contention reflects the same kind of 'patternism' from which Birkeland's work suffers. Other settings are perhaps not so uncertain as Eaton indicates.

5.   *The similarity of the psalms supports seeing them as coming from a restricted royal setting*. This indicates a misunderstanding of the nature of psalm language which is quite general to allow for universal application. This is why it is difficult to detail the setting for some psalms.

6.   *Birkeland's work is commended as an aid in seeing some psalms as a clear unity*. This is clearly not an argument for a royal interpretation so much as a result of it; it begs the question.

7.   *The 'I' and 'we' do at times alternate in these psalms and this can be explained with the figure of the king* but it can also be explained with the concept of a fluid corporate personality. That is to say that the individual was seen as a part of the community in Israel. This also explains the data.

8.   *There are royal elements in the individual psalms such as a special relation to Yahweh and martial language*. This perhaps emphasizes the special relationship with Yahweh too much and ignores the fact that others also have such a relationship in Israel. There is also a form-critical question here. Must such elements always be applied to a king? Is not 'democratizing' to be taken seriously? The martial elements of the language give only slight support to Eaton's position. Eaton takes the view that 'democratizing' is not obvious in these psalms; royal elements indicate a royal psalm unless shown otherwise. The problem is, in part, whether these 'elements' *are* always royal.

9.   *As royal psalms, these compositions can be seen as consistent and meaningful wholes. Otherwise, the royal elements cause problems in interpreting the texts*. When we understand the nature of corporate personality and of psalm language, this may not be so. In any case, it again uses a conclusion arising from the investigation as evidence to support its main thesis.

10.   *There is a considerable gap in Israel's psalmody without this royal interpretation*. The problem with this argument is that the collection of the Psalter in the Old Testament is a late one; it is surprising that any royal psalms are included. They are probably here because they were interpreted messianically.

11. *It fits the royal picture of the Old Testament to see the king as both exalted and humiliated at times as in these laments; this conforms to the ancient Near Eastern understanding of kingship.* This claim suits Eaton's royal interpretation but it does not confirm it. Others could also be exalted and humiliated in their relationship with Yahweh.

Thus, though at first glance Eaton's arguments for his position look impressive, when considered individually, they do not show as much as he claims for them; they do not assure the royal interpretation. Eaton also claims that his interpretation is to be preferred because of the failure of other attempts to find the cultic setting for these psalms. While it is true that some other arguments have failed and none give a setting for all the laments, some of the settings are probably to be accepted for some psalms.[12] It is not necessary to put all the psalms in one setting, nor is it likely to be possible, but a royal interpretation is not required to give the psalms a cultic context. With all this in view, Eaton's arguments leave something to be desired. They almost leave us with the suspicion that he believes a royal interpretation will be helpful in obtaining a clear and full picture of the royal ideal in Israel and that such a picture is possible. Thus he takes the view that the interpretation is virtually assured and, without real success, develops his thesis in order to justify this claim. Further comment on Eaton's work must wait for the treatment of particular psalms.

On the whole, then, the royal interpretation of these psalms is far from assured as a means of categorizing them for comparison and study.[13] The language makes it quite difficult to determine the particular situations from which many of them come and this includes situations of national, or military, or royal distress. These psalms are sufficiently similar in form, content and function to be considered as a class of laments. As has been suggested, this is the best way to proceed methodologically.

Chapter Two

INDIVIDUAL LAMENTS

We now return more explicitly to the topic of prophetic elements in the Psalms. In our survey of the work which other scholars have done on this topic, we saw that significant attention has been given to the oracular elements in the Psalter. These texts have usually been numbered among the prophetic elements in the Psalms, and have sometimes been related to the individual laments and the certainty of a hearing. However, this connection has not been examined in detail even though it is one of the more important aspects in the study of the lament psalms and their relation to prophecy. The study of these texts is thus central to our concerns and the treatment which follows will be directed towards an attempt to delineate what constitutes a prophetic element in a psalm and thereby to broaden the question beyond the consideration of whether an oracle is present in the psalm.

Psalm 31

Our treatment of these psalms will begin with those in which there is a fairly simple expression of the certainty of being heard. We will start with Psalm 31 of which something first needs to be said about its cultic setting. As is well known, Hans Schmidt has proposed that certain psalms are to be understood as prayers of falsely accused persons.[1] The setting proposed is found in I Kings 8.31,32 and is that of a temple trial in which a falsely accused man pleads with Yahweh for his acquittal. The psalm is his plea. Walter Beyerlin has interpreted these psalms in a similar way though with more detail.[2] As we shall see later, there are some psalms which seem to fit this reconstruction of a cultic trial but there are a number of problems with this stimulating proposal. Perhaps the major difficulty is the extent to which one applies the hypothesis; that is, how many psalms can be put in the category. This is a problem because the extremely general language of many of the psalms described as prayers of falsely accused persons, especially by Schmidt, simply does not lend itself to that kind of institutional interpretation. At the same time some of these psalms, such as Psalm 31, do apparently present the speaker as falsely accused. In these cases what is needed is some kind of interpretation between the institutional setting proposed by Schmidt and a purely metaphorical understanding which fails to take into account the cultic setting of the texts as well as the fact that the enemies do actually appear to be false accusers.[3]

Such a setting can be found without great difficulty. It is inevitable in any culture that persons indulge in gossip and malicious backbiting, a kind of slander that cannot be dealt with in the legal system. This would fit the requirement of offering a background in which the enemies are false accusers of a sort but not in the legal sense favoured by Schmidt.

Such malicious gossip would have been a much more serious thing for the person at whom it was aimed than might be thought today, if words were considered to be a powerful force. To be attacked in this way would be likened to total defeat and living under curse rather than blessing. It was much more than simply being embarrassed; the accused person would be in a state of shame and disgrace. Shame indicates a life of dishonour, a broken life without power, and even total destruction.[5] Such a situation would have been taken seriously as something to be avoided in Israel. Men desired to live under blessing rather than curse, and if a person were put in this situation of shame, he would desire a reversal of fortunes and seek to return to the fullness of life under blessing.

Malicious gossip is roundly condemned in the Old Testament tradition. This is true of the book of Proverbs (10.18; 11.13;[6] 20.19) as well as Jeremiah (6.28; 9.3,4) and Ezekiel (22.9; cf. Psalm 101.5). Also important in this connection is Leviticus 19.16 concerning which Brevard Childs has noted an early concern in Israel to protect the reputation of one's fellow against abuse, such as idle rumours, which could cause him injury.[7] These texts indicate that malicious gossip was a serious problem at times in Israelite society.

It was also the kind of problem which Israelite law was inadequate to handle. The Old Testament itself recognizes that the law is not able to deal with all situations which arise in society. It does not cover everything; indeed there are several places where situations arise not covered by the law and new provisions have to be made to deal with these circumstances (Num. 9.6-14; 27.1-11; 15.32-36).[8]

There is also the requirement of two or three witnesses to convict a person of a crime (Deut. 17.6; 19.15) and there must inevitably have been situations in which that number of witnesses could not be found; common gossip or accusations would fit into this category. The function of the witness and especially the problem of false witness was taken very seriously in Israel (Ex. 20.16; 23.1; Deut. 5.20; 19.18f.; Prov. 12.17; 14.5,25). This must certainly have been a problem in Israelite society which could reduce the effectiveness of the law. Further, the law is shown to be inadequate in another, more significant way. The Old Testament documents in several places the use of means other than those of the legal court to determine guilt (Ex. 22.10ff.; Deut. 21.1-9; Prov. 18.18; I Sam. 14.36-46; Jonah 1.7; Num. 5.11-13).[9] Vindication or guilt is here determined in a nonlegal way;[10] the decision comes from Yahweh in each of these cases. He represents a place of appeal when the law could not deal with the situation (Ex. 22).[11] He is judge and ruler over all things so it was only natural that the Israelite would take recourse to Yahweh (the sanctuary?) when there was a problem the law could not solve. The kind of serious difficulty stemming from malicious gossip as it is envisioned here clearly fits into that category.

This is the background which is being suggested for the interpretation of Psalm 31. There is some subjectivity involved in this proposal but its main advantage is that it fits the language of the psalm. The worshipper is hounded and persecuted, in dire straits and falsely accused, but not in any legal way, to judge from the language of the text. Thus it is logical to conclude that he is accused in another way, that of malicious gossip leading to the grave circumstances for the worshipper which are described in the lament. So he appeals to God for relief.[12]

We now turn to Psalm 31. Vv. 2f. indicate that the worshipper seeks protection in the temple from a situation characterized by shame (אבושה, v. 2):

> In you, Yahweh, I have sought refuge.
> Let me never be put to shame;
> deliver me in your righteousness.
> Incline your ear to me; save me quickly;
> be a rock of refuge for me, a strong fortress to save me.

The psalm continues with an expression of trust based on Yahweh's past deeds:

For you are my rock and my fortress;
so lead me and guide me for your name's sake.
Take me out of the net which they have hidden for me,
for you are my refuge.
Into your hand I entrust my spirit;
you have redeemed me, Yahweh, God of faithfulness.
I hate[13] those who pay regard to vain idols,
but I trust in Yahweh.
I will rejoice and be glad for your unchanging love
because you have seen my suffering; you have taken heed of my
  distress.
And have not given me up to the hand of the enemy;
you have put my feet in a broad place.[14]

In v. 10 we return to petition and lament:

Be gracious to me, Yahweh, for I am in distress;
my eye wastes away in sorrow,
my being,[15] even my inmost part.
For my life is consumed with grief and my years with sighing;
my strength fails in suffering and my bones waste away.
I am the object of reproach from all my adversaries and a distress[16]
  to my neighbors
and an object of fear to my acquaintances; those who see me in the
  street flee from me.
I have passed from memory as one who is dead;
I have become like a broken vessel.
For I have heard the slander[17] of many—terror on every side!
as they scheme together against me, plot to take my life.
But I trust in you, Yahweh;
I say 'You are my God'.
My times are in your hand;
deliver me from the power of my enemies and my persecutors!
Cause your face to shine upon your servant;
Save me in your unchanging love.
Yahweh, do not let me be put to shame for I have called upon you;
let the wicked be put to shame; let them perish to Sheol.
Let the lying lips be silent,
which speak arrogantly against the righteous in pride and contempt.
How abundant is your goodness which you have stored up for
  those who fear you,
you have done for those who seek refuge in you before the sons of
  men!

> You have hidden them in the shelter of your presence from the
>   conspiracy of men;
> you have concealed them in your shelter from the strife of tongues.

This prayer is clearly a petition uttered in the context of trust; the fact that the expression of trust is present does not move the psalm into the category of thanksgiving.[18] The crisis is clearly present. The psalm is also understood as a unity here; it has two parts running along similar lines.[19] Petition and trust are expressed in both parts, vv. 1-9 and vv. 10-21, though the circumstances of the worshipper are described in more detail in the second. The unity of the psalm is also supported by the fact that neither section is complete without vv. 22ff., as will be demonstrated below.

To be more specific concerning the situation of the worshipper, he is clearly accused and forsaken. We may note the reference to tongues in v. 21 (cf. also vv. 12, 14, 19).[20] Gunkel and Schmidt relate the accusations to sickness[21] but the references seemingly related to sickness apparently note the result of the crisis rather than its cause (primarily vv. 10f.). It appears more likely that the lamenter is suffering under the curse of malicious gossip, especially in view of the references to false accusations mentioned above. The use of דבת רבים in v. 14 makes this highly probable. There is also the description of the situation as one of shame (בוש) in vv. 2, 18 (cf. v. 13).[22] The vaunted language of the psalm certainly tallies with the significance of such a situation of shame and disgrace as given in the introduction to this *Sitz im Leben*. The accusers are most likely malicious gossipers and this gossip would appear to be the cause of the shame.[23] This explanation would also account for the secret plots the worshipper mentions (v. 13).

There was, no doubt, provision made for such a situation in the cult, as this psalm would indicate. As the lamenter seeks a reversal of fortunes and thus tries to stop the slander against him and obtain relief from his shame, he pleads for Yahweh to give him a cultic sign of vindication to show his innocence. This would bring the worshipper back into the fullness of life and it would also probably mean that his enemies, his accusers, would be placed under the curse of shame. This is what the petitioner begs Yahweh to grant.[24]

An indication that such a sign is granted comes in the expression of certainty in vv. 22f:

Blessed be Yahweh!
for he has wonderfully manifested his unchanging love to me in a
  besieged city.
And I had said in my alarm, 'I am cut off from your sight',
but you heard the sound of my supplications when I cried to you
  for help.

We have already noted that these verses are preceded by an expression of trust, but there is a definite change here to a hymnic flavour with the introductory phrase ברוך יהוה כי (cf. Ps. 28.6).[25] This phrase is injected to express the joy of the worshipper in his newly found certainty. It is God's חסד for which he is praised, God's faithfulness toward the lamenter even in the midst of crisis. The verse carries the implication that this expression of חסד was amazing, even incomprehensible, to the worshipper. This is the means of the answer alluded to in v. 23.[26] In v. 22 the poet uses the figure of the besieged city to describe his crisis. The phrase בעיר מצור has been considered by many to be suspect (cf. *BHS*). However, it is retained in the translation above as a metaphor for the place or time of persecution.[27] Additional support for this viewpoint may be found in a comparison of the phrase with the somewhat similar לי לצור מעוז in v. 3.[28] The worshipper desires a protecting fortress in the midst of this siege.

V. 23 gives a clear contrast of the worshipper's weak faith during his crisis and the fact that Yahweh has heard him. The petitioner is now certain that God has been gracious to him and heard his prayer. This verse with its contrast of past and present also interestingly puts this expression of certainty plainly in the context of the whole psalm. The worshipper is now experiencing the divine presence which he desired during his crisis (cf. vv. 17, 20f.). The protection for which the worshipper yearns in vv. 4-6 is also reflected in the language of protection used in vv. 22f. which relate to vv. 8f. with the use of חסד there and the contrast in v. 9. These considerations support understanding the psalm as a unity. So these verses bring the psalm together in a positive expression of certainty that God has answered the worshipper in his crisis and gives him protection.

There are varying opinions as to how this certainty came about but since the psalm is understood as a lament, the view that an oracle of salvation has been imparted to the worshipper is probably the best option; this is the opinion of Gunkel and Mowinckel,[29] and would indicate that the help is assured or promised rather than in the past.

In any case, the worshipper has been helped and perhaps vindicated
in the midst of his crisis. This action might also include the downfall
of his enemies (cf. vv. 17, 18).

Psalm 31 then concludes with a final exhortation in vv. 24f. It may
well be that this instruction is given by the worshipper to his fellows
in the congregation in the hope that they can also be encouraged
because of his own deliverance:[30]

> Love Yahweh, all (you) his saints; Yahweh protects the faithful but
>   abundantly requites whoever acts haughtily.
> Be strong and let your heart take courage, all (you) who wait for
>   Yahweh!

Psalm 28

Psalm 28 has already been mentioned and its inclusion is appropriate
here because its expression of certainty is similar to that found in
Psalm 31. Psalm 28 evidently relates to a situation similar to that of
Psalm 31; the lamenter is being persecuted and slandered and
hounded by accusers (cf. v. 3). Thus he needs to be shown to be
innocent by Yahweh, presumably in a way other than a legal trial
which would surely have been used if possible. If such a sign of
innocence is not forthcoming, he may well be counted among the
wicked, as his persecutors no doubt say he should be, and suffer the
same terrible fate as they do (vv. 1, 3); this is what he fears.[31]

However, there is a definite change of mood at v. 6. The expression
of certainty begins there:

> Blessed be Yahweh!
> for he has heard the sound of my supplications.
> Yahweh is my strength and shield; in him my heart trusts.
> Thus I am helped and my heart rejoices and I give thanks to him
>   with my song.[32]

The expression again begins with the hymnic phrase ברוך יהוה כי (cf.
Ps. 31.22). These verses also declare that Yahweh has heard the
worshipper and that he offers protection and refuge for him; note
that they follow immediately from the assertions in v. 5b. V. 6b is
also important as it clearly refers back to v. 2 where the poet pleads
for Yahweh to hear his supplications for favour. Vv. 6f. in using the
same terminology (cf. also Ps. 140:7) declare that those prayers have
been heard and answered. The verb שמע indicates that the petition
has been granted; the worshipper has received God's favour.

V. 7 exhibits a vocabulary of refuge with עזי ומגני and ונעזרתי. This reflects the protection the suppliant receives with the answer to his prayer. The verb בטח shows that the worshipper now trusts in that protection. The last part of v. 7 constitutes a vow of praise and the thanksgiving continues from there. Vv. 8f. then continue the emphasis on God's protection. With such a conclusion, vv. 6-9 have a decided hymnic character from beginning to end:

> Yahweh is the strength of his people[33]
> and he is the saving refuge for his anointed.
> Save your people and bless your heritage;
> shepherd them and carry them forever!

Some have suggested that these last two verses betray the psalm as a royal composition.[34] They do widen the context of the psalm to include the king and people, but only as a means of seeing the worshipper's experience in the context of the community.[35] The petitioner desires that the community experience the blessing he has encountered in lamenting to God. As described above in reference to Psalm 31, he has moved from the curse of living under false accusation to the blessing of wholeness of life with Yahweh and his community of faithful persons. The verbs הושיעה and וברך in v. 9 would indicate that he desires the same for the community in such situations.

It is most likely that the certainty expressed in this psalm refers to future protection and deliverance. Mowinckel speaks of anticipatory thanksgiving[36] while Anderson calls it a present reality of faith.[37] A number of suggestions have been made to explain the presence of this sudden change of mood. Because of the similarity to Psalm 31 and the suddenness of the change, some type of institutional explanation is most probable.[38] Mowinckel attributes it to an oracle by a priest or cult prophet.[39]

Pss. 28 and 31 then both speak of the certainty that the worshipper's prayer is heard and that he is protected by Yahweh in the midst of his crisis. This is perhaps the simplest expression of certainty in the laments. But both of these psalms may also imply that included in this protection is the destruction of the wicked (cf. Ps. 28.4f.). Another group of psalms moves toward making this explicit.

Psalm 9-10

The first of these is Ps. 9-10. For quite convincing reasons, these two

psalms are generally taken as a unity.[40] Most of these reasons have
to do with the traditions in which the psalm has been transmitted.
However, it must be said that the two sections of the unified
composition fit together rather awkwardly.[41] As is clear from the
text, the first part is a song of thanksgiving while the section in Ps.
10 is an individual lament. It is unusual, though not unique (cf. Pss. 27;
40), to have a thanksgiving song before a lament. Commentators
have tried to explain this in various ways.[42] However, Mowinckel
may well be right in seeing the composition as a lament starting with
a laudatory hymn.[43] Arnold Anderson suggests that the introductory
thanksgiving may well carry the implied plea of asking Yahweh to do
again what is recounted in the thanksgiving.[44] It is quite difficult to
go beyond that analysis of the form to reach the particular
circumstances reflected in the psalm. The first part has a communal
aspect while the second part appears to deal with an individual.[45] It
may well be that some kind of corruption and oppression by persons
of power is behind Psalm 10.

In such a situation of 'domestic corruption', wicked people are
dominating affairs in society and boasting about it. The little people
are being oppressed by powerful and rich persons, perhaps corrupt
officials; the helpless and poor are being exploited. Such a social
problem has many facets to it—injustice, bribery, and other forms of
corruption and oppression. While there is clearly such a communal
aspect to the problem, there is also an individual component. In Ps.
9-10 the worshipper is evidently one of the oppressed persons, one
among many in a similar situation. He cries out to Yahweh for help,
for justice rather than corruption. He pleads with his righteous God
to enact his judgment for he knows this will bring the appropriate
punishment upon the evildoers. A place would naturally be provided
in the cult of ancient Israel for such a plea as this, since the situation
certainly existed at times and Yahweh was seen as the special
protector of the helpless and the supreme judge of all. Israel's cult
clearly appears to have been related to all such circumstances in life.

This kind of corruption is often mentioned in the Old Testament.
It is found in the legal codes (Ex. 22.21-24; 23.1-9; Lev. 19.11f.). The
prophets also frequently condemn social oppression (Amos 2.6,7;
4.1,2; Is. 10.1,2; Jer. 5.26-29). It is clear from these texts that injustice
was a familiar problem at times for the Old Testament community.
The Psalms also appear to condemn such practices, though in a
different way as in Ps. 9-10. Indeed, it would be odd if such a state of

affairs were not accounted for in the Psalter since it is so noticeable in other parts of the Old Testament.

Ps. 9-10 clearly bears witness to this setting; it uses quite traditional language to describe it (cf. 9.10, 19; 10.2, 8, 9, 13,[46] 18). This is a much more natural interpretation of the text than seeing the language as simply exaggerated expressions of need. A word of caution is in order, however, for it is difficult to move beyond the suggestion of domestic corruption to a more specific suggestion concerning the *Sitz im Leben* of the psalm because of the vague nature of its language.[47]

The psalm ends in the tone of the certainty of a hearing:

> Yahweh is king forever and ever;
> the nations perish from his land.
> Yahweh, you have heard the desire of the meek;
> you will strengthen[48] their heart(s);
> you will make your ear attentive
> to give justice to the forsaken and oppressed,
> without anyone again frightening men from the land.[49]

In keeping with the stereotypical nature of the language in the remainder of the text, this is quite a general expression of certainty. The point is that Yahweh has heard the cry of the meek, probably the cry of the worshipper, and he will help them and bring about justice for them. The crisis described in the lament will not be allowed to happen again, v. 18b. The oppressed worshipper is described as meek in accordance with the account of the crisis in the lament section of Ps. 10 (vv. 2, 9, 10, 12, 14) but now Yahweh has hearkened to the desire of the meek.[50] The theme of Yahweh's kingship, which is basic to the content of these verses, is treated in something of a hymnic fashion in v. 16,[51] which introduces the section and may function to help unite the two parts of the psalm.[52] This verse clearly relates to v. 15 and the petition there. Because Yahweh is king, the enemies and oppressors are no longer able to dominate the meek. So here the overthrow of the wicked is explicitly a part of the certainty of a hearing.[53] These verses then primarily describe Yahweh's kingship as powerful but righteous and just. Befitting the use of such traditions elsewhere in the psalm, v. 18 concludes the prayer with an account of the results of Yahweh's kingship.

These verses also tend to provide some evidence of reference to political corruption in the remainder of the psalm. Perhaps the poor are assured of their rights once again with the overthrow of the godless, v. 16.[54] There is certainly a contrast between the fate of the oppressed and the enemies in these verses[55] and a contrast between the circumstances of oppression and corruption and the newly promised circumstances of justice and protection.

Gunkel calls these verses a prophetic picture of the future;[56] Kirkpatrick understands them as confident anticipation of the future.[57] They most probably do refer to the future as indicated by the tenses used in v. 17b.[58] Yahweh has heard the prayer; he will now begin to grant its petition for the downfall of the enemies. This is basically an assurance of the effectiveness of God's kingship. There is, however, little indication of how this mood of certainty came about. Either the movement of faith or an intervening oracle of salvation is possible, but neither is assured.[59]

Psalm 55

Ps. 9-10 speaks of divine protection in terms of justice for the oppressed and mentions the downfall of the wicked. This combination of themes is seen more clearly in Ps. 55 which is a lament of one who is persecuted. There have been various attempts to define the nature of this persecution more closely. Gunkel and Kraus understand the psalm to be two different compositions and relate the first part to slander and shame while the second (vv. 19aβff.) concerns persecution by non-Israelites.[60] Others relate the persecution to political and military strife.[61] However, the language of the psalm seems so general in character as to inhibit speculation about the specific nature of the persecution. It is possible that the persecution could be attributed to a whole corrupt society since the worshipper certainly feels isolated and in desperate circumstances.[62] We can then look at Ps. 55 simply against a background of persecution, by which term we include some kind of distress, trouble, affliction or crisis whether from mental, physical, material or spiritual causes. Enemies such as false accusers or military enemies can cause persecution as can the experience of illness or mental anguish or loneliness. Sin and the absence of God can also bring about feelings of persecution; our definition is thus a broad one, as required by Ps. 55 with its general language. There is just not enough evidence to be more specific about the setting of the psalm and it is important not to read details into its language and impose a specific setting on a text which requires a more general judgment concerning its background. This is particularly clear in the lament section of the psalm (vv. 3, 4):

Hearken unto me and answer me;
I show restlessness[63] in my murmuring.
I am distraught[64] from the noise of the enemy, because of the
    oppression of the wicked
for they cause distress to fall upon me[65] and in anger they
    persecute me.

The psalm continues in a similar vein, picturing the worshipper as
one facing death and describing the enemies in a stereotyped way[66]
until we reach vv. 17ff.:

But I will call unto God
and Yahweh will save me.
Evening and morning and at midday I will complain and moan and
    he will hear my cry.
He will deliver me[67] into safety from the battle I wage for many
    stand against me.
God will hear and he will humble those who dwell in the East,[68]
who do not change and who do not fear God.
They stretched out their hands against those at peace with them;[69]
they violated their covenant.
The words from their mouths were smooth like butter but war was
    in their hearts;
their words were softer than oil but they were drawn swords.
Cast your burden upon Yahweh and he will sustain you;
he will never permit the righteous to slip.
But you, God, will cast them down into the pit of destruction;
men of blood and deceit will not live half their days
but I will trust in you.

This section is rather long and rambling and contains some
obscurities but it still seems to constitute an expression of the
certainty of being heard, though a very general one. V. 17 begins the
section with an expression of confidence, probably contrasted with
the preceding verses by way of the introductory אני having the force
of 'But I . . .'. The verse also offers a contrast to the oppressors who
pay no attention to Yahweh (cf. v. 20) as the worshipper rejects the
escapism he mouthed in vv. 7ff. and turns to Yahweh. V. 18 clearly
expresses the certainty of a hearing, confidence that the petitioner
will be heard whenever he prays[70] and will be rescued from his
'battle', which is taken as a figurative description of the crisis in
which Yahweh is seen as the final arbiter.[71] The references in v. 20
are very difficult to define.[72] Apparently the verse begins a description
of the enemies, people who pay no regard to Yahweh and his

standards. They are further described as unwilling to change.[73] This is presumably the sense of חליפות even though there is no comparable use of the word in the Old Testament. However, that meaning fits what follows as the enemies are called hypocrites; they have not honoured their agreements with those they are persecuting, one of whom is the worshipper.[74] These verses give part of the reason for the certainty of a hearing and the confidence in the enemies' downfall expressed in v. 20.[75] V. 23 is taken by Gunkel to be an expression of self-encouragement[76] and by Kraus as an oracle[77] but there is no reason why it could not be the worshipper's encouragement to his fellow worshippers as a result of his deliverance. V. 24 indicates that the enemies are consigned to Sheol suddenly (cf. v. 16)[78] and the psalm ends with a final expression of trust. So these verses express confidence and trust and evidently foretell the destruction of the lamenter's enemies[79] but there is little indication of how this certainty might have been achieved. This psalm, therefore, more explicitly combines the certainty of being heard with the fall of the wicked; both concepts seem to be involved in Yahweh's answer to the worshipper's plea. This combination is perhaps even more clearly seen in Ps. 6.

Psalm 6

Here the worshipper is facing a crisis of major proportions; he is at the point of death. It is not easy to determine what the crisis involves but it may well revolve around sickness.[80] Klaus Seybold has recently taken up that possibility and though he classes the reference to sickness as uncertain, he leans to the view that the worshipper is sick and that the psalm is to be placed in a rite of penitence in a domestic setting rather than in the sanctuary.[81] This suggestion seems to carry little weight. Though the worshipper is experiencing God's anger, there is little of penitence in the psalm. There is, however, some support in the text for the view that the petitioner is sick. The key is in verse 3 but vv. 6-8 are also relevant. These are a part of the first eight verses of the psalm in which petition and lament impressively alternate:

> Yahweh, do not punish me in your anger
> or chasten me in your wrath.
> Be gracious to me, Yahweh, for I am languishing;
> heal me, Yahweh, for my bones are troubled.
> And I am greatly dismayed

but you, Yahweh—how long?
Turn, Yahweh, deliver me;
save me for the sake of your unchanging love.
For there is no remembrance of you in death;
in Sheol who will give praise to you?
I am weary with my sighing;
every night I drench my bed with tears;[82]
I flood my couch with my weeping.
My eye wastes away from grief;
it grows weak because of all my foes.

In these verses the lamenter petitions Yahweh to turn to him and
to cease from being angry with him, to heal him and to deliver him
from his enemies. Though they are not mentioned until v. 8, the
enemies must be considered as a part of the problem and may be
connected with the apparent sickness described here.[83] The view
taken here basically follows Mowinckel on the cultic setting of a
psalm referring to sickness.[84] Though it is unlikely that sickness here
is related to sorcerers as Mowinckel suggested, the worshipper would
have sought purification in a cultic ritual and offered prayer there.
Mowinckel understands the ritual to include fasting, putting on
sackcloth and ashes, falling prostrate on the ground, vows, penitential
rites and other cultic purification rites. Sickness would have been
dealt with in this way because it was understood to be judgment from
Yahweh as the above verses indicate, and psalms such as Ps. 6 were
used in the ritual.[85]

There is clearly a change of mood after v. 8 though the enemies
referred to there are still in view:

Depart from me, all (you) evildoers,[86]
for Yahweh has heard the sound of my weeping.
Yahweh has heard my supplication;
Yahweh has accepted my prayer.
All my enemies will be ashamed and greatly dismayed;
they will turn back; they will be shamed in a moment.

These verses expressing the certainty of a hearing begin with an
introductory imperative addressed to the enemies followed by the
particle כי and are clearly set off from the remainder of the psalm.
Kraus speaks of this section as the divine word that the worshipper
has been awaiting in the sanctuary, God's favourable decision toward
him.[87] Kraus also understands שמע (יהוה) to have a formulaic character pointing to the certainty of a hearing in the Psalms. The point of the

verses is that the petitioner has been heard; he has been accepted and experiences God's grace. The verb שמע is often used to indicate that Yahweh has paid attention to the worshipper and granted his salvation, heard him favourably.[88] Notice in v. 9 that it is the lamenter's weeping which has been heard (cf. v. 7). This clearly relates the expression of certainty to the situation at hand and also indicates both the seriousness of that situation and the dialogical nature of the worshipper's faith. The expression of certainty here also includes the downfall of the enemies. They are overthrown suddenly and decisively. Because the lamenter has been heard by Yahweh, the enemies now experience a crisis similar to the one the worshipper has experienced; the situations are reversed. Briggs notes the emphasis of the last two verbs in v. 11; the enemies are turned back in defeat.[89] This reversal of plights between the lamenter and his enemies is further emphasized with the use of ויבהלו מאד in v. 11 and נבהלו מאד in v. 4 (cf. נבהל in v. 3).[90] It is difficult to identify the enemies with any precision, though they are described as פעלי און (v. 9), and are evidently personal enemies. They are only mentioned in vv. 8, 9, 11 but are clearly involved in the distress though it is not clear whether they are its primary cause or are secondarily involved and simply make it worse.[91] What is clear from v. 11 is that the enemies are totally shamed and confounded and rebuffed. It is striking that they play such a prominent role in the expression of certainty but are only briefly mentioned in the remainder of the psalm. This would indicate significant involvement in the crisis at hand. Mowinckel relates their downfall to healing[92] and healing is probably implicit in these verses showing the divine response to the petitions in vv. 2-8 but the relationship between this healing and the enemies is not made clear.

One of the important considerations in the treatment of these verses concerns the tenses used. The address to the enemies in the imperative (v. 9a) is followed by a perfect, apparently indicating that the prayer has been heard and answered. The same form is repeated in v. 10a but the parallel verb is in the imperfect as are the verbs in v. 11. It is unlikely in this context that the verbs in v. 11 would carry a jussive force. It may well be that the imperfect in v. 10b, which is parallel to a perfect, refers to a past event. This event, the acceptance of the prayer, is, however, incomplete;[93] that is, the effect of that past action continues into the present.[94] Could it be that the perfects used here are what have traditionally been called 'prophetic perfects'? In this case the perfect tenses are used to refer to future events, even though the events are viewed as completed in the mind of the worshipper. This seems probable and supports the view that these verses express assurance that the worshipper's prayer has been answered and that the enemies will fall.[95]

There have been several attempts to account for the occurrence of these verses in Ps. 6. Seybold gives three options.[96] (1) They could come from the inner movement of faith. (2) It may be that the worshipper has been delivered (healed) and then these verses were added.[97] (3) It is possible that a *Heilsorakel* was delivered between vv. 8 and 9.[98] Though he is satisfied with none of these options, Seybold considers the third alternative to be the best of them.

Ps. 6 has moved us quite clearly to the view that the divine reply to the worshipper's prayer in the sanctuary includes the downfall of his enemies. This plays an even more significant part in the expressions of certainty of some other psalms. We will begin with Ps. 36.

Psalm 36

In this psalm the worshipper is seeking protection from oppressors, as several commentators have concluded.[99] From its language, some kind of refuge seems to be the most probable setting for it. The view taken here is that the psalm is a prayer for asylum in the sanctuary. The institution of asylum is well attested in the Old Testament though there are apparently two kinds of refuge, one in the (local) sanctuary or at the altar (Ex. 21.12-14; 1 Kings 1.50; 2.28) and the other in the cities of refuge (Num. 35; Deut. 4.41-43; 19.1ff.; Josh. 20). It may be the case that at least at one time these cities were also seen as sanctuaries.[100]

The institution apparently worked in the following manner. An accidental homicide occurs and, because the killer faced death automatically as a result of the accident, he could seek asylum in order that his innocent blood might not be shed.[101] This refuge may have been in the local sanctuary at an earlier period, and later the cities of refuge took over this function. At the specified city, the killer then presented his case to the elders who were to decide whether the killing was accidental. If found innocent of premeditated murder, the person seeking refuge was given a place to stay in the city of refuge until the death of the present high priest. If the killer was found guilty, he faced execution. Though the texts are not exactly clear at this point, there appears to be an initial asylum to allow the trial to take place (Lev. 24.12; Num. 15.32-36). In any case, the asylum granted is a temporary one, primarily in order to allow a trial to take place to ensure justice, an important part of the process. Even a further time of residence in a city of refuge is not indefinite, as has already been indicated.

The passages noted above only deal with the problem of unintentional manslaughter, but it has been suggested that asylum may have applied to a wider variety of acts; the others simply not being given in the text.[102] Since the laws in these passages certainly are incomplete, this conjecture seems quite conceivable and even reasonable; but it is certainly speculative. However, even if this is not the case, the right of asylum must be considered to be a well substantiated legal practice in the Old Testament.

Since many of the sources describing this institution are late, the historicity of the asylum procedure has come into question, but most recent interpreters seem to think it was a historical practice in Israel.[103] It certainly seems to have all the earmarks of an early Israelite practice, even if not always in the developed form found in the passages in Numbers, Deuteronomy, and Joshua, all of which have taken their present form relatively late. A number of psalm interpreters have found a place for the right of asylum in their work[104] but Delekat has most consistently interpreted psalms in light of this institution, seeing many texts as pleas for the right of asylum in the temple or the extension of that right.[105]

Psalm 36 is most likely a plea for asylum. It begins with a description of the evil which is at hand:

> The utterance of transgression to the wicked is in the midst of my heart;[106]
> there is no fear of God before his eyes,
> for he flatters himself in his own eyes
> finding his perverseness to hate.[107]
> The words of his mouth are wickedness and deceit;
> he has ceased to act wisely, to do good.
> He devises evil upon his bed;
> he places himself in a path that is not good;
> he does not repudiate evil.

Though in some ways this psalm is different from many laments, its description of the wicked is reminiscent of other psalms.[108] The wicked pay no regard to Yahweh (cf. Pss. 10.4; 14.1; 64.7) and speak and act wickedly (cf. Ps. 10.7). This typical description of the wicked is then contrasted sharply with hymnic praise of Yahweh in vv. 6-10:

Yahweh, your unchanging love extends to the heavens,
your faithfulness to the clouds.
Your righteousness is like the lofty mountains,
your judgments like the great deep;
you deliver man and beast, Yahweh.
How precious is your unchanging love, O God
and the sons of man take refuge in the shadow of your wings.
They feast from the abundance of your house
and you give them drink from the river of your delights.
For with you is the fountain of life;
in your light we see light.

The contrast is clearly set forth in v. 6 (cf. Pss. 57.4, 11; 108.5).[109]
In v. 8 we have the first clear indication of an interest in refuge. חסד is
still the subject but the refuge בצל כנפיך would most likely have
referred originally to some cultic institutional context; the worshipper
is speaking of refuge in Yahweh. Especially with the reference to a
meal in the sanctuary in v. 9 and eating and drinking there as the
source of life, some kind of refuge in the sanctuary seems to be the
matter before Yahweh in this prayer.[110] This is taken further in the
petition to which this hymnic section leads, and for which it gives the
base (vv. 11, 12):

Continue your unchanging love to those who know you
and your salvation to the upright of heart.[111]
Do not let the foot of the arrogant come upon me
nor the hand of the wicked expel me.

This is a plea for protection, safety and security which, along with
the importance of the theme of protection in vv. 6-10 and the fact
that the worshipper is closely pursued and persecuted, would appear
to indicate a *Sitz im Leben* for Ps. 36 in accordance with the practice
of temporary asylum outlined above. The petitioner pleads for
deliverance from the wicked described in the first section of the
psalm.[112] This protection is envisioned with the expression of
certainty in v. 13:

There[113] the evildoers[114] have fallen;
they have been hurled down and will never be able to rise again.

This verse also offers a contrast to the petition; the enemies
described in the first part of the psalm will experience a fate which is
opposite from that which they no doubt expect; they will fall never to
rise again. Several commentators point to the finality of this downfall

and to the use of the perfect נפלו.[115] The overthrow of the enemies, here described as פעלי און, is one way for the worshipper to receive the protection and salvation he requests positively in v. 11 and negatively in v. 12. It appears that the evil prepared by the wicked (vv. 2-5) for the righteous again falls back on the enemies themselves in a complete reversal of fortunes. The wicked will never have the power to be enemies again. This may be implied from יכלו which can mean 'to have power' and קום which can be used to denote enemies (cf. Pss. 3.2; 27.12, often in participial form). Overthrow of the enemies implies that protection for the righteous is now assured.[116] The final verse almost carries an element of glee at the fall of the wicked. The perfect tense used here may well have the significance of what has been called the 'prophetic perfect' and the downfall be anticipated, as Kirkpatrick suggests.[117] There is clearly a change of tone with v. 13, though it fits well after v. 12, to conclude the psalm on a positive note and pull together this varied composition. The words of the hymn in the psalm will now come to fruition.

Psalm 7

Psalm 36 clearly sees the downfall of the enemies as the primary focus of the certainty of a hearing. This is true with perhaps even greater intensity in Ps. 7 which is a prayer of a falsely accused man, and in this case it is probable that the psalm has an institutional setting.[118] It has already been noted that Hans Schmidt first proposed that a group of psalms were prayers of falsely accused persons.[119] Walter Beyerlin has also supported a similar classification of some psalms and described the institution in the following manner. The purpose of the trial is to arrive at a divine judgment concerning an accusation brought against a man. The person who is accused comes to the temple requesting admission to the sanctuary to plead his case before Yahweh. A preliminary investigation follows, after which he may be admitted into the sanctuary. Such admission to the temple implies innocence but it is only inside the temple that the actual pleading is done and the definitive divine decision made known to all.[120]

The Old Testament does provide textual support for this kind of institution (cf. particularly Deut. 17.2ff.; 19.16ff.;[121] Jer. 26; II Chron. 19.5ff.). Such an institution probably functioned as a court-like procedure in Israel to determine judgments in particular cases. There is also support for the contention that there were sanctuary trials and investigations connected with them (for example, Deut. 13.12ff.) and temporary asylum to allow a trial to take place. Further support is found in the fact that injunctions against false witness (Ex. 20.16; 23.1; Deut. 5.20; cf. also Prov. 25.18 which is reminiscent of some of the descriptions of the enemies in the lament psalms) refer to court situations and in the fact that Israel understood Yahweh as a judge who pronounced verdicts (for example, Zeph. 3.5). Such an institution, therefore, is well documented for Israel.

However, as we have already seen, not all psalms of falsely accused persons fit this kind of institutional context; it is only when their language reflects an institutional, legal background that a psalm is to be considered in this light. Several clues to this setting are found in Ps. 7; the psalm begins with a request for refuge (vv. 2, 3):

> Yahweh my God, in you I have sought refuge;
> save me from all my persecutors and deliver me;
> lest they tear me apart like a lion,
> dragging me away, with no one to deliver.

There immediately follows the oath of self-imprecation or protestation of innocence (vv. 4-6):

> Yahweh my God, if I have done this,
> if there is wrong in my hands,
> if I have requited my friend with evil,
> or robbed anyone persecuting me without cause,
> let the enemy pursue me and overtake me
> and trample my life[122] to the ground
> and lay me in the dust.

In vv. 7ff. the worshipper is pleading for a just verdict in a style like that of the judgment doxology, and clearly makes use of legal terminology:[123]

> Arise, Yahweh, in your anger;
> be lifted up against the fury of my persecutors;
> awake, my God[124] who has commanded judgment.
> Let the assembly of the peoples surround you
> and over it return on high.
> Yahweh judges the peoples;
> judge me, Yahweh, according to my righteousness and according to
>   the integrity within me.
> Let the evil of the wicked vanish but establish the righteous,
> you who test the heart and inward parts, righteous God.

My shield is with God
who saves the upright in heart.
God is a righteous judge
and a God who passes sentence every day.[125]

Then comes the description of the enemy (vv. 13-17):[126]

If he does not turn, he sharpens his sword;
he bends his bow and he prepares it.
He has prepared his deadly weapons,
making his arrows fiery shafts.
Look, he brings forth wickedness
and is pregnant with trouble
and gives birth to lies.
He has excavated a pit and dug it out[127]
but he will fall into the hole he has prepared.
His mischief will return upon his (own) head
and his violence descend upon the crown of his head.

The last two verses are particularly important here and give
expression to the certain downfall of the enemy. Vv. 11f. have already
begun to indicate a positive tone of trust and vv. 13-15 begin to show
the inevitable failure of the wicked. The preparation described there
comes to naught in vv. 16f. It is here that the certainty of a hearing
actually comes to light, though these verses are organically connected
to vv. 13-15.[128]

The enemies have been described with metaphors[129] and are now
compared to hunters in vv. 16f.[130] They are hunting with a trap they
have excavated. However, rather than the worshipper, who is the
intended prey, falling into the pit, the enemies themselves fall in. The
picture is elaborated in v. 17. Gunkel finds the origin of this idea in
the picture of a stone falling back on an enemy's head.[131] These
pictures are frequently employed in the laments; the evil the enemies
prepare for the righteous returns upon the heads of the enemies
themselves. Weiser even calls this a well-known legal maxim in the
ancient Near East.[132] It should be said here, however, that it is
Yahweh who accomplishes this reversal of fortunes. He is faithful to
his word and in that word the enemies are seen as destroyed. The
reversal of fortunes is clear from the remainder of the psalm. The
petitions uttered in vv. 2f., 10 have been answered and the judgment
requested carried out. The oath of self-imprecation in vv. 4-6 has also
now been executed on the enemies rather than on the worshipper, as
the dust and ground there are also a part of the picture in vv. 16f.

Yahweh has done his judging and testing and the results are now made known. In addition the enemy has not turned (שׁוב, v. 13) but the evil has now turned upon him; he has truly brought forth his own trouble (vv. 15, 17, שׁוב; cf. Ps. 55.11). The reversal of fortunes is quite important in this psalm and emphasizes the contrast between the righteous and wicked.[133] Briggs calls ישׁוב in v. 17 the imperfect of future expectation;[134] the enemies' downfall has not actually occurred yet but is clearly assured. God's judgment has been determined and the worshipper's prayer for deliverance answered. The psalm then concludes with a vow of praise and thanksgiving (v. 18):

> I will give thanks to Yahweh according to his righteousness
> and I will sing praise to the name of Yahweh Most High.

Schmidt has claimed that it is so amazing that the first part of this psalm and the last are in one text that there must have been a favourable decision granted the petitioner;[135] but the way in which such a decision would have been revealed is not made clear in the psalm. Nonetheless it is clear that the worshipper's prayer has been answered and the fall of the enemy predicted, with that fall taking the form of a returning of his plans upon his own head. A similar theme is found in Ps. 57.

Psalm 57

A number of suggestions have been made concerning the setting of this psalm.[136] Schmidt[137] and Kraus[138] understand it as a prayer of a falsely accused man and Beyerlin goes further in placing the psalm in a set procedure in the cult.[139] The text is recited in the refuge of the sanctuary the night before judgment is expected to come; the prayer is a plea for a positive verdict from God. In opposition to this view, it must be said that the language of the psalm is too vague to posit such a specific institutional setting. Anderson has suggested that the language may be more metaphorical.[140] And yet it is evident that the worshipper seeks some type of judgment, probably in a non-institutional sense.[141] This is seen in the first part of the psalm (vv. 2-6):

> Be gracious to me, God, be gracious to me for in you I have sought
>   refuge
> and in the shadow of your wings I seek refuge until destruction
>   passes.

> I call to God Most High,
> to God who accomplishes (his purpose) for me,[142]
> He will send from heaven and save me; he will reproach those who
>   trample upon me.[143]
> God will send his unchanging love and faithfulness.
> I am lying in the midst of lions who are furious with the sons of
>   men;
> their teeth are spears and arrows and their tongues sharp swords.
> Be exalted above the heavens, O God;
> let your glory be over all the earth.

The worshipper is pleading for protection in the temple (v. 2 cf. Ps. 7.2). In the last half of v. 3 he expresses confidence in the God he is appealing to, the God who judges and decides between the righteous and the wicked. This sentiment immediately leads to what may be an expression of certainty in v. 4, but the situation is not totally clear since the imperfects here could carry a jussive force.[144] However, the perfect חרף is also found, though it fits into the verse rather awkwardly.[145] Hence it is also possible that the verse expresses confidence rather than a wish. Since God is to reach out 'from heaven', it may be that a theophany tradition is reflected here. God's messengers חסד and אמת are to deliver the worshipper from his enemies (cf. v. 11).[146] God will prove his dependability. With verse 5 we are thrown back into lament and then petition in v. 6. V. 5 (cf. Ps. 7.3) makes it probable that the lamenter has been falsely accused and that the text is to be understood in the context of the setting described for Ps. 31; it is a non-institutional prayer of one falsely accused. This section then concludes with v. 6 which is reminiscent of the judgment doxology found in Ps. 7 (cf. vv. 10-12 here which also have a similar tone as the psalm ends with a repetition of v. 6). The judgment which is requested in v. 6 is then carried out in v. 7:

> They prepared a net for my steps; I was bowed down;
> they have dug a pit in my path but they will fall into it themselves.

There is a significant contrast within the verse. Once again the destruction the enemies prepare for the worshipper is returned upon their own heads. In the last part of the verse the downfall of the enemies is certain. They have set a trap in the path the worshipper is to take, but their evil returns upon their own heads with the force of a boomerang.[147] Though the figure of speech in the verse certainly refers to hunting, falling into the pit could also indicate going down to Sheol.[148] The perfect tenses used here certainly refer to the future and anticipate the enemies' doom.[149]

It may be that an oracle has brought about this certainty of a hearing but it is also conceivable that the certainty could have come in faith since the entire psalm seems to have a certain amount of confidence underlying it and the expressions of confidence fit well into the psalm's structure and movement. Following the expression of certainty in v. 7 the worshipper moves immediately to thanksgiving, rejoicing and praise,[150] and so the psalm ends in a splendid expression of the vow to praise Yahweh.

The certainty which is expressed in Ps. 57 is again primarily concerned with the downfall of the enemies and is expressed with the concept of their evil returning upon their own heads which is now seen as a significant part of the complex of ideas in the laments and particularly the divine response to them. This feature is also seen in one last individual lament, Ps. 64.

Psalm 64

Most commentators relate the setting of this psalm to a crisis brought on by slander and accusations by enemies.[151] Kraus,[152] Delekat,[153] and Beyerlin[154] all also relate the psalm to the right of asylum in the sanctuary. It is clear that the worshipper is persecuted by many enemies who use secret plots against him (vv. 2-7):

> Hear my voice, O God, when I complain;
> preserve my life from fear of the enemy.
> Hide me from the secret plots of the wicked,
> from the scheming crowd of evildoers
> who sharpen their tongues like swords,
> who prepare[155] bitter words as arrows
> to shoot at the innocent from ambush,
> shooting at him suddenly and without fear.
> They hold fast to their evil word;
> they talk of laying snares thinking, 'Who can see us?'[156]
> They devise injustices, 'We have completed a shrewdly conceived
>   plot'.
> For the inward mind and heart of a man are deep.

V. 4 makes it clear that words are the weapons of the enemies (cf. v. 9; Ps. 57.5).[157] However, the language of the psalm seems to militate against placing it in the setting of an institutional prayer of a falsely accused person,[158] though v. 5 (cf. Pss. 7.16; 9.16; 140.6) indicates that the worshipper is innocent. What he needs is some type of sign to show publicly that this is the case, and so it seems likely that this psalm should also be understood in the light of the same background as Ps. 31.

There is then an abrupt change of tone and the worshipper is suddenly delivered from the arrogant enemies he fears (vv. 8-11):

> But God will shoot them with (his) arrow;[159]
> suddenly their defeat[160] will come
> and their tongues[161] will cause it[162] to fall upon them.
> All who see them will wag their heads.
> Then all men will fear
> and will declare God's act
> and will ponder what he has done.
> Let the righteous rejoice in Yahweh and seek refuge in him;
> let all the upright in heart glory.

These verses present a striking contrast to the rest of the psalm.[163] The positions of the worshipper and enemies are once again reversed in what is clearly an expression of the certainty of a hearing. Anderson[164] and Kirkpatrick[165] note the public character of the triumph of the worshipper over the enemies, again perhaps giving some indication of the setting for the psalm. In v. 8 God shoots, or shoots at, the enemies and their downfall is sudden.[166] Then the effect of this judgment is narrated.[167] The arrogant wicked are publicly humiliated, since the significance of v. 9 is apparently one of scorn.[168] The mention of tongues in v. 9 should also be heeded for the identification of the enemies; their lies have caused their downfall. As has been noted, the reversal of fortunes is again important and this is expressed again with the concept of the enemies' evil returning upon their own heads. The relationship between evil and judgment is seen with the arrow and the tongue (cf. vv. 4f. and vv. 8f.). This is perhaps one of the less immediately explicit expressions of this concept and yet most powerful; it is clearly at the heart of the psalm. This sudden and surprising downfall of the enemies is seen by others who heap scorn upon them, so that the enemies are humiliated and dishonoured. The sequence of events provides an important witness to God's power and providence to wake up the people. Consequently these verses affirm God's rule; people will now consider him and not disregard him in arrogant power as did these enemies (v. 10 which perhaps moves into the area of a vow). The faithful rejoice and give thanks for this judgment and its effect in the final verse. The downfall of the enemies is certain and so the worshipper is now protected as he requested in vv. 2f. It may be that this psalm forms a kind of prophetic announcement of judgment on the wicked and that such judgment on the enemies, in this case most probably false accusers, is portrayed here.

Since the movement to v. 8 is quite sudden, an oracle could have come at this point in the ritual but it is difficult to be sure.[169] The tenses probably indicate a future frame of reference in this context.[170] It is the sudden downfall of the enemies as a result of the return of their evil upon them that is at the fore in the expression of certainty in this psalm and, indeed, in the last four psalms discussed.

Conclusion

In the treatment of these psalms it has become clear that one of the primary concepts in the set of ideas found in the expressions of certainty in the individual laments is that of the protection of the worshipper. This was communicated in various ways, the most basic of which was the joyful expression of the certainty that the worshipper's lament has been heard, perhaps best understood as proximity to divine presence. These expressions were often connected with language concerning protection (Pss. 28; 31). In several psalms this certainty of being heard was also combined with the downfall of the enemies, another way of protecting the lamenter (Pss. 6; 9-10; 55). The sudden fall of the enemies was the major concept used in the final group of individual laments treated and this was expressed in terms of the evil the enemies prepared returning upon their own heads (Pss. 7; 36; 57; 64). So though the primary means of communicating it may differ, the concept generally at the fore of the expressions of certainty in the individual laments is that of protection for the worshipper[171] pointing to the important theological assertion that Yahweh is a god who helps persons in these situations of crisis and lament. With this similarity of content as well as the clear connections in form and vocabulary, it is now assured that the certainty of a hearing is a uniform phenomenon in the individual laments and can be considered both as a whole and as an important element in these psalms.[172] However, as has been shown above, this phenomenon can be associated with varying *Sitze im Leben*.

In the introduction to this chapter, we noted that the expressions of certainty in the individual laments have often been related to the oracular element in the Psalms. While it may well be that the *Heilsorakel* is the most probable explanation for the presence of this certainty, this cannot at present be considered assured, and it is noticeable that none of the expressions treated above actually takes the form of an oracle but rather that of response to some divine word of assurance. The expressions of certainty in the individual laments are not oracles though the two may be somehow related. However, it has been shown that these expressions of certainty do most likely refer to the future and predict the downfall of the enemies and divine help for the worshipper; this is evidenced in the tense structure and the context. Since such assurance and judgment is understood to come from Yahweh himself, these expressions of certainty are quite similar in intent, if not form, to prophetic speeches of weal and woe. In this sense they may be called a 'prophetic' element in the Psalms. If it be objected that this definition is too general and that a call to repentance should be a part of anything prophetic, it may be countered that a number of texts in the Prophets do not call for repentance and that the word 'repentance' should also perhaps include the movement from doubt and discouragement to trust in divine deliverance (cf. Pss. 6; 9-10; 31). Another question which might arise is that of the prophet's experience leading to his utterances. It should be sufficient to say that often we know very little about such experiences and, in any case, some kind of experience and communication from Yahweh must be behind the expressions of certainty treated above. Hence, neither of these objections should keep us from understanding the certainty of a hearing in the individual laments as a 'prophetic' element in the Psalter in the sense of anticipating deliverance and judgment.[173] Ps. 64, the last text treated above, is a good example at this point since it forms a kind of prophetic announcement of judgment on the wicked which is perhaps protrayed in a cultic manner in connection with the psalm.

It is important to note that it is not the identity of the cultic functionary who delivered the expression of certainty, nor any type of assurance leading to that expression, which determines that the text has a prophetic character.[174] It is rather primarily the function which the language of the text conveys and that function in this case can be considered prophetic in the sense defined above. However, it is important to note that the function in this case is also clearly in a liturgical context rather than an explicitly historical one. So the function of the certainty of a hearing in the individual laments in

Israel's cult is to anticipate deliverance for the worshippers and the downfall of the enemies.

Chapter Three

COMMUNITY LAMENTS

To complete our analysis of lament psalms, we will look at some of
the communal laments. These psalms are important in the discussion
at hand for two primary reasons. The first is that they show a more
direct relationship to the oracular form often associated with prophecy;
examples of oracles are present in these psalms. The second reason is
that these psalms confirm with clarity the conclusions drawn from
the individual laments in the last chapter. The same basic element of
psalmody is present in perhaps an even more explicit way.

As with the individual laments, the first psalms to be treated in this
chapter will be those in which certainty in Yahweh's protection of his
people is affirmed. This may best be understood as a concrete and
experiential manifestation of Yahweh's חסד, his unchanging love.
This term was encountered in the first psalm treated in the last
chapter, Ps. 31 (v. 22). It is the חסד of Yahweh which is the moving
force behind the deliverance experienced there. This had been
requested in v. 17 (cf. v. 8). The same concept is used as a motivation
for deliverance in Ps. 6.5 and is particularly praised in the hymnic
section of Ps. 36 (vv. 6-10). This forms the basis for the plea that this
חסד may continue towards those who know Yahweh (v. 11). It is also
God's unchanging love which is his messenger to effect deliverance
in Ps. 57.4. Thus, Yahweh's חסד plays a significant role in the
expressions of certainty in the laments. While the English words
'love', 'mercy' and 'grace' may all be included in this concept, it
appears best to define it as unchanging or steadfast love because it
affirms the fact that God's choice out of love of his persons and
people does not change with the circumstances of life (cf. Is. 40.6). In
spite of the crisis at hand, God's love and relationship with the
worshipper(s) does not change, but continues. The worshipper(s)
needs in his present circumstances to be shown that this is still the
case. It is in the ritual of which the lament psalms are a part that this
חסד is experienced in a renewed way for the worshipper(s); it is seen

as re-enacted and still functioning in the present. Thus this unchanging love is basically understood as God's loyalty to his people. He is faithful to his promise to deliver, which means that his commitment to his people does not change as circumstances do. So this clearly is coupled with the theme of Yahweh's faithfulness which is also found in these psalms (Pss. 31.6; 36.6; 57.4).[1] This in turn calls for faithfulness from the people in response to this renewed demonstration of Yahweh's חסד for them (31.24f.; 55.23).

While it would be unwise to limit the understanding of Yahweh's חסד to a covenantal framework,[2] especially with the current difficulties in dating the beginnings of Israel's understanding of Yahweh as a covenant God, the term does include Yahweh's unchanging loyalty to his covenant people. God's prior love for his people is now still operative in a loyal and unshakeable fashion. Thus the term in the lament psalms does seem to indicate a relationship between Yahweh and his people, however that is conceived, and a relationship to which Yahweh is intensely loyal. In this חסד he delivers those who know him as is confirmed in the songs of thanksgiving (for example, Pss. 107; 118; 136).

Psalm 12

Demonstrations of God's protection of his people by way of his חסד are also seen in the community laments. This kind of protection is not always expressed with the term חסד but the theme is still present. This is seen first of all in Ps. 12, the setting of which is reflected in its initial plea (vv. 2f.):

> Help, Yahweh, for the godly have vanished;
> for the faithful have disappeared[3] from among the sons of men.
> Everyone utters lies to his neighbour;
> they speak with flattering lips and a double heart.

The worshipper is facing a completely corrupt society. Gunkel speaks of the ruling class oppressing the poor, perhaps after the exile[4] and Weiser's suggestion of general decadence in influential circles from which the worshipper suffers reflects the mood of the text.[5] Such is clearly the general conflict and there is no need at all to see the text as post-exilic; it is a cultic cry to Yahweh in the midst of societal corruption in some ways not unlike that described in Ps. 9-10, though here primarily seen from the communal viewpoint. Mowinckel relates the psalm to the New Year festival possibly in a

time of alien rule.[6] The next two verses continue the plea arising
from this setting:

> May Yahweh cut off all flattering lips,
> the tongue making great boasts,
> those who say, 'With our tongue we will prevail;
> our lips are with us; who is our master?'

Mention is often made of the לשׁון and שׂפה of the enemies in the
laments (Pss. 31.14, 19; 57.5; 64.4, 9; cf. Pss. 14.1; 36.2, 4; 55.4, 22).
This is indicative of their arrogance even in relationship to Yahweh.
They feel secure in their oppression of the poor. Following this plea is
a clear change in the mood of the text (vv. 6f.):

> 'Because of the oppression of the poor, because of the moaning of
>   the needy,
> now I will arise', says Yahweh;
> 'I will place (him) in the safety for which he pants'.[7]
> The words of Yahweh are pure words,
> silver refined in a furnace on the ground,[8]
> purified seven times.

There is clearly a change in voice and form in v. 6 since here
Yahweh is speaking directly in a kind of oracular form. The text is
difficult but the meaning is generally clear. The poor and needy
described are those faithful who are responsible for this plea to
Yahweh and are being oppressed by the arrogant wicked described in
the first four verses. The oppressors may be those in high places but
it is difficult to identify them specifically. Yahweh here describes that
he will arise and place the needy (the worshippers in this ritual) in
safety from the oppression they are suffering. Yahweh will deliver
them as they have shown in their petition that they desire to be
delivered. Yahweh says that he will arise (cf. Pss. 7.7; 9.20; 10.12;
17.13; 94.16 and especially Is. 33.10); he will now become the
superior enemy of the wicked (cf. above on Ps. 36.13). However, in
v. 6 this is expressed positively in terms of Yahweh's deliverance of
the needy and v. 7 affirms the trustworthiness of this word from
Yahweh. It is completely pure (purified) in contrast to the words of
the enemies (vv. 3-5). So these verses are once again about Yahweh's
protection of his people. Buber points out that the psalm is built
around a vision of the beginning of God's intervention against the
lying generation. He points to the עתה of v. 6 as prophetic in the sense
that salvation is now being actualized; these verses give a prophetic

vision of judgment and deliverance from a present crisis[9] and are then clearly to be seen as a prophetic element in the psalm since they anticipate God's deliverance of the worshippers. The first part of the expression of certainty is also in oracular form and calls the worshippers to repent from any despair and doubt they are experiencing in this crisis. Anderson suggests that the oracle was spoken by a priest or cult prophet with the rest of the psalm by the congregation.[10] Kraus speaks of v. 6 as Yahweh's unmediated speech inspired as prophecy and relates it to the salvation oracle tradition and the beginning of the theophany in the cult. Here an actual salvation breaks into a crisis which seems hopeless. The worshipper will now be put in the sphere of salvation, ישׁע, as Yahweh is loyal to his word even in the midst of hopelessness.[11] The salvation here is anticipated but clearly assured. Yahweh affirms this and the congregation responds to it in v. 7.[12] So these verses clearly have a prophetic function in this community lament. The fact that the protection for God's people is anticipated is seen in the conclusion of the psalm which again refers to the 'sons of men' in v. 2:

> You, Yahweh, do protect them;
> preserve us from this generation forever.[13]
> The wicked prowl around on every side,
> as evil is exalted among the sons of men.

Ps. 12 constitutes another cultic demonstration and re-enactment of Yahweh's חסד for his people as it clearly anticipates his protection of the worshippers. Though the function is clearly prophetic in the sense defined above and even with the use of an oracular form in v. 6, the psalm is still clearly cultic rather than referring to an identifiable historical context. The language of the psalm itself precludes that kind of specificity. So Ps. 12 speaks in the cult in a prophetic way of Yahweh's protection of his people.

Psalm 126

This theme of God's protection of Israel even in the midst of need is also sounded in Ps. 126 though apparently in a different setting. There are three basic options for the setting of this text. The first is that the psalm comes from the Autumnal Festival and is a prayer to assure Yahweh's blessings for the new year.[14] Kraus relates the text more clearly to the historical setting of the time after the exile in which the restoration has taken place but the great prophetic

promises for that restoration have not.[15] Finally Gunkel takes the
view that the whole psalm is forward looking and refers to God's
great victory in the end-time.[16] We will consider the text of the
psalm before making a final decision concerning its setting. The first
three verses are important in this matter:

> When Yahweh restored the fortunes of Zion
> we were like those who dream.
> Then our mouth was filled with laughter and our tongue with
>   shout(s) of joy;
> then they said among the nations, 'Yahweh has done great things
>   for them'.
> Yahweh has done great things for us;
> we are glad.

The meaning of the first verse is crucial. Is the phrase שוב שבות[17] a
technical term referring to the eschatological end-time[18] or does it
refer to the deliverance from the exile or is it simply a more general
phrase indicating God's restoration of his people?[19] The translation
given above is the more general one which seems to fit this context
better as we will see below and as is appropriately reflected in
Anderson's commentary.[20] The remainder of these verses narrate
the response to God's restoration or deliverance of Israel which was
so magnificent that the people thought they were in a dream.[21] Note
in v. 2 the reference to the mouths and tongues of the people, here
showing their great rejoicing over this deliverance. This is quite a
contrast to the reference to the enemies' tongues in Ps. 12.4f. Further
response is then put in the mouths of the nations as a witness to
Yahweh's action and greatness and finally Israel rejoices over her
deliverance by God.

Also of significance in these verses is the temporal frame of
reference. Can the perfect tenses here refer to the future and thus
indicate a prophetic oracle as Gunkel contends?[22] Since deliverance
is requested in the second part of the psalm with the same phrase in
vv. 1 and 4, he sees the whole psalm with a future reference and the
first three verses as a prophetic oracle indicating the complete
confidence of the prophet that this will happen. The whole psalm
then becomes a prophetic liturgy combining this oracle with the
following community lament asking that this salvation be actualized.
However, the more likely view is that the first three verses do indeed
look back on some past deliverance and form the basis for the
petition for deliverance from the present crisis.[23] Even on Gunkel's

interpretation, there is a shift from a deliverance perceived as actualized to the request for that to happen in the present, so that his argument against understanding vv. 1-3 as referring to past deliverance loses some of its force. Verses 1-3 are, then, to be taken as looking back on a past deliverance of Israel by Yahweh. On the basis of this past act, the people then plead for salvation in the present (vv. 4-6):

> Restore our fortunes, Yahweh,
> like the streams in the Negeb!
> May those sowing in tears
> reap with shouts of joy!
> He who goes forth weeping and carrying the seed for sowing
> shall indeed come back with shouts of joy, bringing his sheaves
>   (with him).

V. 4 is reminiscent of v. 1 and the restoration mentioned there. Here the restoration requested is also likened to the renewal of the streams in the southern part of Israel. When Yahweh returns the water to them and fertility to the land, it is as if they have been turned from sterility and the control of death to full life and well-being.[24] V. 5 then apparently continues the petition though the verb could be taken as a regular imperfect expressing future confidence, reinforced in v. 6 which clearly refers to hope for the future, hope that Yahweh will repeat the salvation described in vv. 1-3. On the other hand, it may well be that the petition in v. 5 is answered in similar imagery in v. 6. Kraus relates the weeping and sowing to ritual weeping and joy in the lament liturgy.[25] Is the imagery of sowing and reaping a reference to the actual harvest of crops or does the imagery refer to the harvest as a part of the fertility ensured in the New Year festival?[26] Perhaps the latter option is the more probable given the tenor of the entire psalm and its reference to a change of fortunes, fertility and prosperity. Gunkel relates the imagery to Osiris' rising from the grave just as a seed will rise from the ground. Just as he rises from the grave, it is believed that the seed will grow and a bountiful harvest bring joy. This means that the psalm returns to the certainty Gunkel finds in its beginning.[27]

Because of its style, imagery and particular references, Ps. 126 is best understood in the context of the New Year festival, though this does not preclude a possible reference to a specific prior deliverance of Israel as even Mowinckel has suggested.[28] The psalm ends with the expression of confident assurance that Yahweh will bring his people fertility and good harvest in the new year. Hence the ritual once again demonstrates Yahweh's protection for the nation, but it still clearly has a future reference and in this sense the last part of the psalm can be said to be prophetic. Baumann has suggested that the conclusion actually takes the form of a *māšāl* to answer the petition in the same way that the prophets often used this form to express faith that a petition will be answered in the future.[29] This suggestion, if correct, would strengthen our conclusion. The end of the psalm certainly implies a response to the petition, and this is clearly a prophetic dimension in the psalm; but it is important to remember that this does not necessarily dictate the identity of the cult official involved. It is not essential for a prophet to be present to mouth the last verse of the psalm; that can be done in the normal movement of the priestly ritual.

Psalm 85

Another psalm which is related to Ps. 126 and expands the prophetic dimension found there is Ps. 85. The options for setting are similar to those in Ps. 126. Mowinckel sees the psalm in the context of the Feast of Tabernacles[30] as does Anderson who also sees a relationship to the return from exile.[31] Gunkel understands the text as a liturgy with basically the same meaning as Ps. 126 with a reference to God's great eschatological victory.[32] Kraus relates the psalm more specifically to history and the return from exile but also understands it to have an eschatological dimension.[33] The beginning of the psalm (vv. 2-4) is certainly reminiscent of Ps. 126:

> You were gracious to your land, Yahweh;
> you restored the fortunes of Jacob.
> You forgave the iniquity of your people;
> you pardoned all their sin.
> You withdrew all your fury;
> you turned (back) from your hot anger.

In v. 2 we are once again faced with the meaning of שוב שבות. The phrase is taken here once again to refer to the restoration of the fortunes of Israel or of her well-being. Each line basically says the same thing: God has been gracious to his people. The outburst of fury which had overflowed from Yahweh, עברתך, has passed; Yahweh has withdrawn it (cf. Is. 12.1). This signifies a past demonstration of the actuality of Yahweh's חסד in relating to his people in the midst of need. Gunkel understands these verses to express prophetic certainty concerning God's great eschatological victory for Israel and to be spoken at a time when Israel suffers under foreign rulers.[34] However, it is more likely that the verses, with the perfect tenses used, have a past reference. In any case, this does not really help specify the identity of the deliverance mentioned. As with Ps. 126, the language is quite ambiguous and could refer to the restoration from the exile but that is not necessarily the case. The description needs to be seen in the full context of the psalm which continues with petition (vv. 5-8):

> Turn to us, God of our salvation
> and annul your vexation toward us!
> Will you be angry with us forever,
> prolong your anger to all generations?
> Will you not refresh us again,
> so your people may rejoice in you?
> Yahweh, show us your unchanging love
> and give us your salvation.

On the basis of God's past demonstration of his חסד in crisis, of his turning from judgment to favour (vv. 2-4), the poet here pleads with God to renew that חסד in the present situation.[35] God is once again perceived as angry and the plea is that he will once again turn (שוב, vv. 4, 5) from that anger which is here pictured as an active, moving force. The experience of God's wrath has begun to discourage the people and they plead for refreshing, תשוב תחינו, for Yahweh to turn to enliven the people, to quicken and revive them. In other words, the plea is for Yahweh to turn and restore the people to fullness of life in his presence and favour, so that they experience the wholeness he intends. The response to this petition follows in vv. 9ff:

> Let me hear what the God Yahweh will say
> for he will speak peace to his people and his godly ones
> but let them not return to folly.
> Surely his salvation is at hand for those who fear him,
> that glory may dwell in our land.
> Unchanging love and faithfulness will meet (each other);
> righteousness and peace will kiss.
> Faithfulness will spring up from the ground
> and righteousness will look down from the sky,
> Yahweh will indeed give what is good
> and our land will yield its fruit.
> Righteousness will go (swiftly) before him
> and make a way for his (foot)steps.

This section of the psalm begins with a phrase (in the style of Pss. 81; 95)[36] indicating that an oracular utterance is to follow. The speaker here says that he will receive and communicate Yahweh's word to his people; he is inspired to speak Yahweh's word which follows.

It is clear in v. 9 that through his messenger Yahweh will speak peace, שלום, to his people who are his חסיד, his pious ones, that is those who respond to his חסד with loyalty. The picture is one of fullness and completeness in life and is somewhat similar to that of Ps. 126 though expanded significantly. The last line of v. 9 is apparently a warning, as a part of the prophecy of prosperity given in the psalm, that the people are not to return to their erring ways.[37] However, it is clear that Israel's crisis is now effectively past and the people are given hope that God will intervene for them. Anderson surmises that the prophetic utterance may come from earlier oracles of comfort;[38] the language is rather picturesque and formal, but that does not dictate its origin. Thus v. 9 speaks in the third person of God's providing stability for Israel. In v. 10 the nearness of salvation in the midst of crisis is said to mean that 'glory' will again fill the land as a dynamic, living force to effect blessing for the land. This glory was concretized in the temple in pre-exilic Israel and some take this to be a reference to the exile and the departure of God's presence from Israel. That is quite conceivable but not necessary. Glory could be understood to be absent in any major crisis indicating God's absence or wrath.[39] In any case, the presence of God will come to effect well-being for his people.

Then, in the striking parallelism of the following verses, this well-being is put explicitly in terms of unchanging love and faithfulness. Yahweh's messengers or servants are here personified as exemplifying the coming blessings of material and spiritual prosperity,[40] the extent of which is pictured in v. 12; it reaches all creation. Vv. 11, 12 offer a picturesque description of God's coming with שלום, brought about because of God's חסד which brings his people into a right relationship with him. We may note how the faithfulness of v. 11 is picked up in v. 12a and the righteousness of v. 11b in v. 12b. The second of the first pair of words חסד ואמת is used in v. 12a and the first of the second pair (v. 11) צדק ושלום is used in v. 12b. This technique extends the picture of prosperity to give its full expansive effect in v. 12.

The prosperity is pictured in v. 13 in terms of fertility, for it is said that the land will yield its increase. In the first line of the verse, this is phrased as Yahweh's giving what is good and it is concretized in the second half of the verse as a good harvest, the produce of the land which Yahweh has given to his people. It is not uncommon for טוב to indicate prosperity[41] and here it is defined more closely. In the final verse of the psalm this prosperity is described in terms of the presence of God with the people, in a right relationship with each other. Yahweh comes to his people as he is faithful to them and they are to him. The faithfulness is reciprocal. Yahweh will give them the prosperity they seek in seeing that their soil will give the deserved return for their labour; and Yahweh will do this in his righteousness. Thus A.R. Johnson sees Ps. 85 as perhaps an early reminder to the people of God of חסד ואמת and its outcome in righteousness as this was seen in the context of the Sinai covenant and perhaps it is a formal reminder of Israel's responsibilities in the covenant.[42] That aspect of the psalm is present but its primary function is to offer assurance and certainty of Yahweh's protection for his people. The oracular element here clearly does that. These verses paint a picture of the peace and welfare which Yahweh promises his people. Mowinckel describes them as a promise of 'victory and happiness and welfare and fertility for land and people and royal family and all classes; of Yahweh's favour and of peace and good crops and of doom and annihilation for the enemies of Israel and all evil powers . . .'[43]

So once again an oracular element in a psalm speaks of Yahweh's protection and promise of prosperity for his people. With the images used and description of that fertility and well-being, it is most likely that this psalm also belongs to the festal complex of the New Year and the plea for prosperity in the middle section of the psalm and which is promised in the last section is based on the prior deliverance of Yahweh narrated in vv. 2-4. It is conceivable that this deliverance is return from exile but with the ambiguous language used that is quite difficult to specify. This general language supports the cultic understanding of the psalm which clearly has a prophetic element in the last section promising prosperity for the people. It is in oracular form, as in Ps. 12. It further calls the people to a commitment to that promise of well-being from their righteous God of חסד. The description of this demonstration of Yahweh's חסד is similar to that of Ps. 126 and serves a similar function, but the description in Ps. 85 is much fuller and relates to an oracular form. This form, and the anticipatory function of the text, do not necessarily indicate the office of the speaker in the cult though the officiant would most naturally be a priest, as mediator of Yahweh's blessing to the people.

In summary, we have seen that Pss. 12; 126; 85 all promise Yahweh's future protection of Israel which is certain in the view of the worshippers. In Pss. 12; 85 this promise assumes a more oracular form and calls the people to trust in Yahweh that he will accomplish his word, that he will protect his people in their times of need.

Psalm 14

The prophetic expressions of certainty in the community laments also express the anticipated protection of the people coupled with the downfall of their enemies. This combination is particularly seen in Ps. 14 which has a setting and background similar to Ps. 12 in which all of society is seen as totally corrupt and Yahweh's faithful cry out for his greatly needed intervention, as in the first four verses:

> The fool says in his heart, 'There is no God'.
> They act corruptly; they do abominable deeds; there is none that
>   does good.
> Yahweh looks down from heaven upon the sons of men
> to see if there are any who act wisely, who seek after God.
> They have all gone astray; they are all alike corrupt;
> none of them does good, not even one.
> Have they no understanding, all the evildoers
> who eat my people as they eat bread,
> who do not call upon Yahweh?

This section contrasts the description of the נבל and his godlessness with a picture of God who looks down to test the children of men and who finds that they are all corrupt. A significant study of the mixing of wisdom and prophetic elements in Ps. 14 has been undertaken by Robert Bennett who understands vv. 1-3 to reflect the wisdom style and vv. 4-6 a prophetic style describing oppression and God's intervention.[44] The psalm is a sustained commentary on the נבל, based on the wisdom theme of the consequences for a community with godlessness in its midst. Such sin and sacrilege disrupt the order of God's community as it disregards his חסד. The consequences of such acts follow immediately upon them and here the wise uses the נבל as a negative example for teaching purposes. He acts against God's חסד and the demonstration of that unchanging love. So the text serves as a prophetic warning against this kind of practical

atheism. Weiser also notes the prophetic character of the psalm.[45]
Here one should compare Is. 5.8ff.; Jer. 5.1ff., 12f.; 8.6ff.

V. 4 presents an interesting conclusion to this picture of godlessness
which permeates the foundations of human life. The verb ידע also
relates to wisdom and understanding. Do these evildoers have no
knowledge? This kind of rhetorical question performs the function of
an accusation against the wicked who are said to eat Yahweh's people
as bread. Gunkel identifies the wicked as the priests who eat offerings
and lead the people astray and cause them to stumble, and sees Ps. 14
as a post-exilic prophetic warning directed against such priests,[46] but
it is more likely that the phrase refers to slander and evil words, and
indicates that the oppression of the wicked is as commonplace as the
eating of bread.

However, with v. 5 we have a significant change:

> There they are in great terror
> for God is with the generation of the righteous.
> You would confound the plans of the poor
> but Yahweh is his refuge.

Here we have a picture of God's intervention in the situation
beginning with שם to show the effects of that intervention. This usage
should be compared with Ps. 36.13, an individual lament where the
particle שם performs the same function in the expression of the
certain downfall of the enemies.[47] Yahweh is here pictured as
sustaining his faithful community by way of his vindicating presence
so that the fools, arrogant and disregarding as they are, are now in
great fear. This is a significant contrast to the preceding description
of them.[48] This fear apparently refers at least to their fall from
previous dominance. This seems the most likely interpretation of the
verse, which is an expression of faith that God will save his
community. It thereby presents a prophetic look into the future.[49]
The psalm has moved from doubt to certainty with the perfect tense;
God has intervened for the righteous and as judge of the wicked.[50]
The contrast with the fall of the evildoers is continued in v. 6 where it
is seen in terms of the intention of the wicked to confound or
frustrate the plans of God's faithful. However, Yahweh himself
prevents this by intervening and protecting the righteous as a strong
protector or refuge. The psalm then ends with a final plea for Israel's
deliverance from Zion and a vow of praise:

> Oh, that Israel's deliverance would come from Zion!
> When Yahweh restores the fortunes of his people
> let Jacob rejoice and Israel be glad.

This petition to make the salvation real indicates what the believer can expect in the future[51] and makes clear that the deliverance previously described is an anticipated one. Note that the deliverance comes from Zion, the place of Yahweh's presence and judging, and that this deliverance is again described with the phrase שוב שבות, another indication of its general reference to Yahweh's restoration of his faithful community.

Ps. 14 is thus a good example of the use of different traditions, here wisdom and prophetic, clearly within the realm of the cult. Those traditions are used to describe the lamentable situation and the protecting and judging intervention of Yahweh in this liturgical context. They are not applied to a specific historical context and do not define the functionaries proclaiming the wisdom and prophetic aspects of the text. They are all used in a unified way in the context of the normative cult of Israel and its purposes of worship, where the leaders seek to help the worshippers actualize God's intervention to save in such a time of need. The expression of certainty here still anticipates protection for the faithful by Yahweh but it moves further in also anticipating the downfall of the wicked in a more explicit way in v. 5.

Ps. 14 is repeated in Ps. 53, the only real difference being in the expression of certainty in v. 6. The text varies significantly:

> There they are in great terror, (in) terror which has not been,
> for God has scattered the bones of the one who encamps against
>   you;
> you will put (them) to shame for God has rejected them.

This also contrasts clearly the former glory of the wicked with their current plight of destruction. Their bones are scattered even without burial.[52] The verse seems to refer to a more definite occurrence than the expression of certainty in Ps. 14.[53] Though there have been various attempts to reconstruct an original text and account for the changes here in such a manner, perhaps the text has been changed to fit another circumstance.[54]

The meaning of the first line is fairly clear. The evildoers are now experiencing a previously unknown terror. Their downfall is made more graphic with a martial figure of speech in the second line. The meaning of the last line is more difficult. The enemies are put to shame, being rejected by God and so destroyed and living under the life of curse rather than blessing. Apparently the text affirms the responsibility of the righteous to put the wicked to shame because of God's rejection of them since this is now decreed and facilitated thereby.[55] This verse fits its context well and its purpose is apparently application to a more specific situation, or at least to strengthen the expression of the certainty of the downfall of the wicked. It is difficult to go beyond this general statement of purpose though it is certain that the fall of the enemies is made more explicit here.[56]

Ps. 14 perhaps more clearly affirms the protection of the faithful but Ps. 53 more clearly proclaims the downfall of the wicked. It anticipates this and is thus prophetic in its expression of certainty. Both lament psalms contain such a prophetic element in anticipating the protection and deliverance of the faithful and the fall of the wicked. They thus call the people to affirm their faith in this eventuality. Both sections are clearly marked off and provide additional evidence for understanding the expressions of certainty in this way.

Psalm 60

A final community lament moves even further into description of the fall of Israel's enemies. Ps. 60 is evidently from a background of military strife and so naturally deals with the national enemies of Israel. We shall see that the structure of this lament is particularly interesting and somewhat different from the others we have discussed. Anderson sees the psalm as a community lament on a day of fasting.[57] Despite some of the national references in the psalm, it is difficult to go beyond this broad cultic situation to put the text in any particular known historical crisis.[58] The psalm begins with a description of the crisis (vv. 3-5):

> O God, you have rejected us, broken out upon us;
> you have been angry; restore us!
> You have caused the land to quake; you have split (it open);
> repair its breaches for it totters.
> You have caused your people to know severe things;
> you have given us wine that made us reel.[59]

Israel is in a fearful situation, one of great danger, in which Yahweh has 'broken out' upon them. This not unusual phrase (cf. Ex. 19.22; Ps. 106.29; I Chron. 15.13; Job 16.14) indicates that the anger of God has confronted them. In this way they are experiencing not so much the absence of God as his judging presence. The result of this divine punishment is the quaking and splitting of the earth or perhaps more properly the land here in reference to Israel's military needs. The second half of the verse moves to a petition for Yahweh to repair, as it were, the breaks in the wall of defence around Israel; the land is about to collapse. Israel has been given the cup of divine wrath (v. 5); they are experiencing suffering or hard times and their very existence is pictured as precarious. The description continues in vv. 6f.:

> You have set up a banner for those who fear you
> (only) to flee before truth.[60]
> In order that your beloved (ones) may be delivered,
> help with your right hand and answer us![61]

The meaning of נס as banner, or standard, is apparently best in this context but it is difficult to be very precise about the reference. Apparently v. 6 means that the banner of Yahweh's people has only served the purpose of leading them in flight from the seemingly victorious enemy. Despite the truth that God is a God of victory, he has allowed this defeat. In v. 7 the beloved refers to the people of Yahweh who petition their God that they might be answered and saved by the power of his mighty right hand which has shown itself to be effective in Israel's salvation history. A significant change then takes place in the psalm (vv. 8-10):

> God has spoken in his sanctuary:
> 'With exultation I will divide up Shechem
> and portion out the Valley of Succoth.
> Gilead is mine and Manasseh is mine
> and Ephraim is my helmet,[62]
> Judah my scepter.
> Moab is my washbasin;
> upon Edom I (will) cast my shoe;
> over Philistia (I will) shout in triumph'.

This is a divine speech in response to the predicament described in the first part of the psalm. It is spoken from the holy place or sanctuary[63] and immediately follows the plea וענני. God proclaims that he will be victorious over Shechem and Succoth and portion them out to his own. Then he moves to the land of his people. Ephraim and Judah are here pictured as Yahweh's special possessions and his rulers. They are triumphant with Yahweh and so rule over Canaan.[64] Then the defeat of Moab, Edom and Philistia is described; the figures of the washbasin and shoe indicate defeat as well as demeaning service.[65]

Thus the oracle offers hope of victory for Yahweh's people. It embraces the entire geographical area associated with the ideal of the Davidic empire.[66] God rules victoriously over Canaan and this is a comfort to his people in this military context. There is a question whether this oracular speech might be an older utterance inserted here and applied to the current situation.[67] That must be considered a significant possibility given the difference in the nature of the oracle and the rest of the psalm and how it almost interrupts the flow of the text. The attempt of Johnson[68] to translate the oracle in a form of direct address to Yahweh carries little weight; the translation given above is quite satisfactory. Following this oracular utterance, there is another change in the structure of the psalm (vv. 11-13):

> Who will lead me to the fortified city?
> Who will guide me to Edom?
> Have you not rejected us, O God?
> God, you did not go forth with our armies.
> O give us help against the enemy
> for vain is the help of man!

Now we have returned to lament which may indicate that the oracle has not come to fruition.[69] V. 11 apparently voices concern that there is no one to lead (meaning Yahweh—cf. v. 12) the people against the enemy, here exemplified as Edom. Then v. 12 returns to the picture seen in vv. 3-5 as a basis for the petition for God's help in v. 13. The plea is that Yahweh will rise up against the enemy oppressing Israel. To this end the psalm concludes on a confident note:

> With God we shall do valiantly
> as he will tread down our adversaries.

The enemies will fall, the military enemies of the nation. Yahweh will trample them under foot, destroy them. He will enable Israel to show great strength in this battle, to perform great deeds of valour. Hence the psalm ends on a note of confidence and certainty in the hope of God's future victory.[70] The psalm then has moved from lament and petition to an oracular utterance offering hope in this time of national military crisis, back to lament and petition and then to a final expression of certainty.[71] This should not be considered as exceptional in the lament ritual in the cult; such sudden changes are not unusual and such alternation of positive and negative viewpoints is also often found in the laments (cf. Pss. 12.5ff.; 22.22f.; 31; 36; 57, for example).

This phenomenon is perhaps seen even more clearly in the setting in which Ps. 60 occurs again in the Psalter, Ps. 108. Here a vow and hymn of praise and thanksgiving from Ps. 57 are attached as an introduction to Ps. 60.7ff. The result is that the psalm moves from that kind of hymnic mood into the petition of Ps. 60 and follows that psalm to its conclusion. This arrangement does provide a more positive tone for the psalm[72] which has apparently been reapplied here to a different situation.[73] For Mowinckel this indicates that oracles can be reused in the cult; they are a permanent feature of the cult with stereotyped patterns. The oracle in Ps. 60 in a situation of war with Edom and other neighbouring nations is applied in Ps. 108 to a new situation. This is apparently the purpose of the change in Ps. 108 and puts the psalm in a more clearly cultic context of confidence in Yahweh.[74]

So this final community lament clearly speaks of the downfall of the enemies of Israel in its various expressions of certainty. It also affirms the rule of Yahweh over the nations. These elements are clearly prophetic in anticipating the downfall of the enemies and the coming rule of Israel for Yahweh. The oracular form is used in this call for the people to move from doubt and despair to hope and assurance for the future. This prophetic function is still clearly in the cult but, we repeat, it does not dictate the identity of the functionary delivering the oracle, which in any case is not the primary question. This psalm and its expression of certainty do, however, further clarify our understanding of prophetic elements in the lament psalms.

Conclusion

In summarizing our treatment of community laments, we conclude that the content of the expressions of certainty found here is quite similar to that of the individual laments treated in the last chapter. In each psalm, Yahweh's חסד is renewed for his people. Pss. 12; 126; 85 speak primarily of Yahweh's protection of his people though in rather different contexts, whether in terms of deliverance or future prosperity. Ps. 14 (53) continues this theme of protection of the nation (rather than individuals within the nation dealt with in the last chapter) but adds to this the theme of the downfall of the enemies. This latter theme is then emphasized in Ps. 60 (108) with the defeat of Israel's military enemies. It is clear from this chapter that the phenomenon of the certainty of a hearing is a uniform one here as in the individual laments. The evidence is too impressive to decide otherwise.

These expressions of certainty have also been considered a prophetic element in these psalms. This is so in the same sense as that given for the individual laments. They anticipate the protection of the righteous and the fall of the wicked. However, in the community laments the oracular form which is often associated with prophecy is more in evidence and this makes the argument for understanding these expressions as prophetic more clear and more certain, and it also means that we may be moving closer to some conclusions as to the prophetic experience behind the expressions of certainty. The oracular form apparently indicates that there has been some experience of Yahweh in receiving his word; though as with much material in the Prophets, the exact nature of this experience is not often specified.[75] Some of the oracles present in these psalms are not dissimilar to the foreign nation oracles found in some prophetic books (for example, Is. 13-23; Nahum; Habakkuk). Finally in this connection, these expressions of certainty do call the people to repentance in the broad sense suggested in the last chapter. They are called to move from doubt to trust in Yahweh's future deliverance. Thus we may categorize these expressions as prophetic elements in the Psalms.

It is the anticipatory function of promise which warrants calling these passages prophetic, but this does not necessarily point to the view that they are the work of cult prophets. They could as easily have been delivered by a priest, just as could the expressions of certainty in the individual laments. It is not the functionary who determines whether a text is prophetic but rather the function of the text. Neither is the form the deciding factor, though it does influence the final decision. Having said that, it is still clear that these community laments refer to a liturgical or cultic situation and are used there, even though historical references may be closer to these psalms than in the case of the individual laments.

It is thus the case that a part of the complex of ideas of the lament psalms in Israel's cult is the prophetic phenomenon of the certainty of a hearing from Yahweh. This is an important element in the cult and one link between it and prophecy.

THE EXPLANATION OF THE CERTAINTY OF A HEARING

It is now appropriate to bring into clearer focus the various attempts to explain the presence of the phenomenon of the certainty of a hearing. Some scholars attempt to explain its presence by assigning it to a different situation from that of the remainder of the lament psalm. This includes understanding the expressions of certainty to be from another psalm or psalm fragment and concluding that these expressions were added later after the worshipper's or nation's deliverance from distress.[1] It also includes the possibility that the psalms were used as a whole in services of thanksgiving rather than lament, a setting which would place the psalm after the deliverance.[2] These suggestions flounder when the language, unity and cultic situations of the psalms are taken seriously.

Other explanations issue from the nature of Israel's cult. Weiser understands the cult to have the purpose of re-actualizing Israel's *Heilsgeschichte* for the present generation. Thus, the expressions of certainty are the results of that process in the lament situation in the cult.[3] J.W. Wevers has related the expressions to the necessary success of the ritual with the invocation of the name 'Yahweh',[4] which carries a kind of magical significance. Both these suggestions raise difficulties of delineating just what they would involve and of whether they really agree with the language of the texts as well as the nature of Israelite religion.

There is also the psychological explanation often associated with Friedrich Heiler.[5] Faith and the nature of prayer are important here. There are sudden changes of mood in prayer which are brought about by the tensions between the actual situation and the ideal, what one hopes for; after all, it is some kind of hope that induces persons to pray. So it is by way of an inner working of faith within the context of prayer that the change of mood to the certainty of a hearing is to be accounted for, according to Heiler. It is true that the expressing of one's lament can bring some relief, but this effect hardly seems enough to account for the expressions of certainty in the laments. The changes of mood are often quite sudden and must be seen in the context of the cult of ancient Israel. Thus it is probable that a more institutional explanation of some kind is in order.

Perhaps the most popular way of explaining the presence of the certainty of a hearing has been to infer a *Heilsorakel*. The basic argument is that during the cultic ritual, a favourable oracle is directed toward the worshipper who has just uttered his lament. The oracle tells him that Yahweh is with him and will help him. Then the worshipper responds gratefully to this oracle with the expression of certainty. This suggestion was first made by Küchler in his work on the use of the oracle to obtain the divine will in Israel.[6] His suggestion has been followed by a number of other psalm scholars.[7]

Probably the most important proponent of this position has been Joachim Begrich.[8] He finds a number of examples of the priestly oracle of salvation in Deutero-Isaiah which he understands to have been borrowed from the cult and lament psalms. The prophet has borrowed this form from the cult to emphasize that God is still Israel's deliverer, even in the situation of the exile. The oracle generally begins with the injunction 'Fear not!' addressed to Israel. When there is no address, substantiating clauses follow immediately, often preceded by כִּי, and usually with a nominal clause such as 'I am with you', expressing the helpful nearness of Yahweh. This would be followed by the assertion that the prayer of the suppliant has been heard, in the perfect tense. Then comes the promise of salvation in the imperfect which is the consequence of the answer to the prayer. The oracle closes with the motive of the hearing and often a repetition of the injunction against fear.

A good example of one of the oracles in Deutero-Isaiah is Is. 41.8-13. The prophet begins in verses 8, 9 with an introduction concerning Yahweh's past acts of grace toward Israel. Then in v. 10 comes the assurance of salvation. There is first the 'Fear not!' and then the substantiating clauses, 'for I am with you' and 'for I am your God'; the verbs are in the perfect. Verses 11, 12, in the imperfect, speak of the fall of Israel's enemies. Yahweh has turned to Israel and now he intervenes on her behalf. Then v. 13 repeats the point of the oracle.[9] Also relevant to both the tradition of the oracle of salvation and Begrich's work is the 'psalm of Hezekiah' in Is. 38.[10] The background of the psalm is clearly one of worship and is usually related to some sort of cultic celebration of thanksgiving, perhaps involving a sacrifice. While the language could easily be used as metaphor for some other kind of dire distress, it is likely that the psalm was intended for use by one who was sick. A setting for such psalms has already been discussed in connection with Ps. 6.[11] The text vividly describes the worshipper's sojourn in the underworld. He is in the worst of situations, most probably at the point of death, and uses a variety of metaphors to cry to Yahweh for help. The psalm concludes with an expression of certainty and vow of praise.[12]

Many scholars understand the 'psalm of Hezekiah' to be a psalm of thanksgiving but it is also possible to classify it as a lament psalm with an expression of certainty.[13] If this were the case, the structure of the psalm would be as follows: lament section (vv. 10-15); petition (v. 16); certainty of a hearing (vv. 17-18); vow (vv. 19-20). The certainty of a hearing and vow tend to merge because vv. 18-19 give the reason for the certainty expressed. Motivations for God to hear the petition are found throughout the text (cf. vv. 10, 11, 14, 15, 16). There is no initial invocation; Fohrer accounts for this by saying that more scope is then given to the lament.[14] This does give the psalm a striking and stark beginning; it moves right to the point.

However, one of the difficulties with seeing the psalm as a lament is the introductory words in vv. 10, 11. These perfects can be translated in such a way that would fit a lament, but it must be said that it would be more natural to understand them as introducing a psalm of thanksgiving. Yet, it is also the case that the literary types of lament and song of thanksgiving are closely related, as has already been noted; it is sometimes difficult to distinguish between the two. For our purposes, the choice made between the forms is not determinative since the *Gattungen* are so closely related.

All of this makes it clear that Is. 38.9ff. is a psalm relevant to our discussion in form, setting, language and also in reference to the certainty of a hearing. The expression of certainty is found in vv. 17f.

> Look, I had great bitterness[15] rather than prosperity;[16]
> but you have brought me back from the pit of destruction with
>   your love[17]
> for you have cast all my sins behind your back.
> For Sheol cannot thank you; death cannot[18] praise you;
>   those who go down to the pit cannot hope for your faithfulness.[19]

This corresponds to the expressions of certainty found in the Psalms. The sudden change of mood is signified by הנה and ואתה.[20] There is a sharp contrast between the crisis and the new assurance of deliverance. The worshipper was in Sheol and is now delivered from the underworld; he has been heard and is in a new situation of trust and relief. V. 17 is crucial for the certainty of a hearing. The verbs are in the perfect, indicating God's certain intervention to save the lamenter from death and Sheol.[21] His bitterness is mentioned because it has been changed into thanksgiving (cf. Is. 12.1). He is brought back to life and forgiven,[22] a process which could include healing. חשקת has often been emended in this verse, but not in the translation given above. The word is difficult in this context but seems to make the point of God's deliverance in a striking way. With the basic meaning of 'being attached to' or 'joined together' the verb speaks of God's presence with the worshipper to deliver—a symbol of his love.[23] Then in v. 18 comes the negative expression of the reason for this deliverance. The dead in Sheol cannot praise Yahweh or hope for his presence and help. Then the psalm continues with the vow of praise. Once again it is made clear that Yahweh's unchanging love has been actualized in a crisis. The point of the verses is God's protection of the worshipper based upon the hearing of his prayer, a primary concept in the theology of the certainty of a hearing. Also it is apparently the case that this expression of certainty is anticipatory (cf. v. 20).

The expression of certainty here, therefore, corresponds to those in the laments of the Psalter.[24]

In Is. 38 the 'psalm of Hezekiah' is placed in the context of Isaiah's ministry during Hezekiah's sickness and carries a prophetic function of offering assurance that Yahweh carries out his word even in crises such as this one. Such a sentiment is expressed in vv. 17f. Even though the setting in Is. 38 has moved away from the cult, the psalm still has that background and this must be understood when attempting to account for the sudden change of mood in the psalm. Here the oracle is the most likely explanation, especially in light of vv. 4ff.; that is certainly the understanding of the redactor in this section of Isaiah. Thus Is. 38 is also a text which strengthens Begrich's argument favouring the salvation oracle as the explanation for the certainty of a hearing in the Psalter.

Begrich has made an important contribution to the question of the explanation of the certainty of a hearing; his case for relating these oracles of salvation to the lament psalms is too impressive to be dismissed. Other, more recent psalm interpreters have been influenced by his work.[25] Other factors also support the salvation oracle as the best explanation for the certainty of a hearing. There are other passages of similar form in the Old Testament;[26] there are also other ancient Near Eastern parallels which seem to reflect this oracle tradition.[27] Some of these texts have a remarkable similarity to Begrich's reconstruction of the priestly salvation oracle. In addition to these considerations, the oracular elements in the community laments have already been noted above as an important part of the lament complex in Israel's cult. Despite the reservations of some scholars, the evidence does support the existence of a salvation oracle in Israel and one related to the lament psalms. However, the caution of Weiser and Kilian at this point is warranted.[28] The oracle of salvation is not a perfectly satisfactory solution to the problem.

One final possibility should be mentioned: the expressions of certainty found in the laments could be a later literary development in the history of the Psalms.[29] This would probably have taken place after the exile when the oracle was no longer in use, and something like the certainty of a hearing theology was needed in the different liturgical situation. It is quite likely that the expressions of certainty were expanded as the psalms were used in worship through the years. Some may have come into existence in this way but it appears more likely from the evidence that they existed in some form in the pre-exilic cult in Israel.

Though somewhat less than ideal, the oracle of salvation seems the most probable explanation for the presence of the certainty of a hearing. At this point it is important to note that this oracle would not have to be delivered by a cultic prophet; a priest could do it.[30] Neither the form of the oracle nor the position of the functionary who delivers it can determine whether it carries a prophetic force. So the acceptance of the oracle as the best explanation for the certainty of a hearing does not in itself warrant the conclusion that the certainty of a hearing attests a prophetic element in the Psalms though it does not weaken the case for that assertion in any way. Understanding the oracle as anticipating and assuring deliverance for the worshipper(s) as well as judgment for the enemies would support the view that the expressions of certainty have a prophetic function. In addition, this view would associate the certainty of a hearing with a form often found in prophetic literature; it was certainly used often by Deutero-Isaiah. This fact is further supporting evidence for understanding the expressions of certainty in the lament psalms as being a prophetic element in the Psalter.

Chapter Four

PSALMIC PASSAGES IN THE PROPHETS

It has long been recognized that there are psalmic passages in the prophetic books. Mowinckel used Habakkuk as an example of this, calling Habakkuk a cult prophet and psalm poet.[1] The Book of Habakkuk is filled with psalmic material, even with the certainty of a hearing. Others have characterized the book as prophetic liturgy;[2] a number of reasons have been given for this, centring on the form and language of the book.[3]

An important part of the treatment of Habakkuk is the beginning of the prophet's message, chapter 1.2-4.

> How long, Yahweh, shall I cry[4] for help and you not hear?
> or cry out to you, 'Violence!' and you not save?
> Why do you make me see wickedness and look upon trouble
> as destruction and violence are before me, as there is contention
>   and strife arises?[5]
> Thus the law grows numb and justice never goes forth
> for the wicked surround the righteous so that justice goes forth
>   perverted.

This lament comes from a situation quite similar to that discussed in connection with Pss. 12; 14.[6] The entire society is corrupt and the current state of affairs appears to be completely uninhibited. The form of the lament is singular but the reference is clearly communal since the person is put into the context of a corrupt society which provides the occasion for the lament. Ps. 9-10 should also be mentioned in this regard and the combination of the individual and community aspects there, as well as in Pss. 12; 14. The prophet is using traditions from the cultic sphere to express his lament; it is probably more accurate to posit this than some kind of direct literary dependence.

A comparison of these verses with the lament psalms makes it clear that they take the form of a lament with the petition inherent in the penetrating questions in vv. 2f. Such rhetorical questions are also found in the Psalter (for example, Pss. 10.1; 13.2f.; 85.6f.). The whole notion that the poet has been crying to God for a long time and that he is surrounded by violence and destruction are part and parcel of the lament tradition.[7] The short lament concludes with the plaintive statement that all order in society is going awry; the wicked are in control so that there is no justice or righteousness.

Then with v. 5 there is a sudden change in the text and God responds to the prophet's lament by saying that he is working in an incomparable way through the Chaldeans to punish this wickedness. Chapter 1, then, begins the prophetic book with psalmic lament and divine response.

A second lament begins with v. 12. The prophet is dissatisfied with the response to the first lament because a righteous God is using an evil, ruthless people to bring about his justice. These verses also partake of the same tradition in structure, language and context as that of the laments in the Psalter, particularly the community laments with military enemies involved (Pss. 60; 74; 79). In the second chapter, God responds to this with promise of a vision and of the downfall of the enemy (v. 5). The remainder of chapter 2 is a series of woes which affirm this positive response to the lament. Again God's unchanging love is renewed for his people, even in the midst of difficulty.

The final chapter of the book is a psalm, even having its own title. It begins with a plea based on Yahweh's past acts for his people. The plea is that these acts be renewed in this time of trouble. The theme is similar to Pss. 85; 126 and perhaps reflects a similar institutional origin. With v. 3 we begin the account of the prophet's vision. The psalm then concludes with an expression of certainty.[8] The poet will confidently wait for God to accomplish his purposes;[9] the verses affirm the certainty of God's protection.[10] Chapter 3 thus functions as a lament with its plea and confident expression of certainty.

The book of Habakkuk partakes of much that is common to the lament psalms. It begins with a lament over corruption in the land,[11] the response to which leads to another questioning lament. The full response to this lament on how a holy and righteous God can allow the evil and ruthless Chaldeans to serve his purpose is confirmed with the psalm in chapter 3. The form and content of the book relate clearly to the lament complex of ideas. The language also has many of the same qualities as that of the Psalter, though it is still clear that the book serves the prophetic function of offering assurance and predicting the initial success but final downfall of the Chaldeans.[12]

It is also the case that the certainty of a hearing plays an important part in the book of Habakkuk. We have already seen that the first two laments receive answers and that these correspond to the expressions of certainty in the lament psalms. The psalm in chapter 3 has been characterized as a lament with an expression of certainty. V. 17 expresses lament and the certainty of a hearing follows. We can also see a relation to the vow of praise in these verses; Hab. 3.18f. express trust and praise for Yahweh.[13] The content of these verses and of the previous oracles in response to the laments in chapter 1 is generally the same as that in the certainty of a hearing in the Psalms. It speaks of victory over the oppressor, whether internal or external, and of protection for the lamenter, which is a fundamental point in the certainty of a hearing in the Psalms (for example, Pss. 10; 12; 28; 31; 55).[14]

Thus a relationship between the laments of the Psalter and Habakkuk is clear; but the question which we must now consider is what conclusions to draw from this relationship.[15] Habakkuk uses the language, form, content, and certainty of a hearing of the Psalter but they are all applied to his situation, which is discernible from the text, at least in its initial frame of reference.[16] The prophet uses the lament tradition, originally cultic, to express his prophecy which has the function of proclaiming that salvation and protection are coming for the people of God.[17] This is the same general function of the expressions of certainty in the Psalter, but here put in a different context, a historical rather than liturgical one. The oracular form is also used for the replies, as is the woe form in chapter 2.[18] The dominant use of the rhetorical question is also a part of that adaptation,[19] and there is the psalm in chapter 3 which is functionally a lament, but which uses a theophanic hymn tradition to offer assurance in the midst of crisis. V. 16, with the response of the prophet to the vision, is also an adaptation of the psalmic material in a mode more common to the prophetic books.

The book of Habakkuk predicts salvation for the faithful and calls upon them to wait expectantly for it. It calls for the repentance of the dominating wicked in Israel and predicts their downfall as well as that of the Chaldeans. The prophet uses traditional, often psalmic, language to give expression to his genuine prophetic experience. The prophet uses these traditions in such a way as to speak the prophetic word to his day, in a historical rather than liturgical context. This

reflects a significant distinction between psalmody and prophecy—
that of adapting function to a specific context, with corresponding
shifts in form. However, it also needs to be said that, in situations
such as those found in Habakkuk, this may be the only real
distinction between the two kinds of literature.

This observation means that it is a mistake to accept the view that
the forms the canonical prophets used were always bound to their
original setting. In the case of Habakkuk, they have clearly been
changed from that of their origin.[20] The prophet used traditional
material to express the word of assurance from Yahweh to the
faithful in his day. Form cannot always be assumed to dictate
function in the prophetic books. A prophet may skillfully use
material that was originally cultic in form, but this does not
necessarily mean that he functioned within the cult.[21]

The title 'cult prophet' is thus inappropriate for Habakkuk. He
rather uses material originally from the cult and applies it to his own
day and prophetic message. The material has been given a historical
context and it is the question of function which clarifies this for us.
This underlines the importance of meaning in the prophet's context
rather than the question of origin of form which helps with understanding but does not resolve the issue. An emphasis on function and
the context of that function is demanded.[22]

A final text we should mention is the book of Joel. Mowinckel has
claimed that Joel was a cult prophet and temple singer.[23] Kapelrud
has advocated the view that the book is a formal liturgy performed in
the temple.[24] A number of Old Testament scholars understand Joel
as functioning within the cult, primarily because of the forms and
terminology used in the book and its positive attitude toward the
cult, including the use of many traditional cultic concepts.[25]

It is difficult to give a precise date and historical setting for Joel,
though several settings have been suggested.[26] On balance we prefer
the position of H.W. Wolff and others which puts the book into the
post-exilic period.[27] While it must be agreed that vocabulary evidence
can be quite tentative, the language used tends to support such a
date.[28] In addition, while the temple mentioned could be the pre-
exilic one as probably as the post-exilic, the description of the cult is
more reflective of the later period. This is also true of the description
of the community. Furthermore, the book uses much traditional material, even from other prophets.[29] The historical allusions in the book
and the attitude toward the cult would also fit this period. These relate

the book to a setting in which Israel has experienced the trauma of exile and has returned and begun to function again as a social community. The people thus look forward to the Day of Yahweh when he will come to bring full restoration and vengeance upon their enemies.

The book begins with a call to lament over a locust plague. It then moves to a description of the crisis in chapter 1.15ff. The language and imagery used would support the view that the problem is one of the destruction of the harvest and the devastation of the land which supports the people and their livestock. This disaster is judgment which is a harbinger of the Day of Yahweh. These verses are fragments of lament rather than full lament songs because they concentrate almost solely upon the description of the distress at hand and so do not contain the other elements of the psalm of lamentation such as petition and vow.[30] V. 15 begins with a cry of woe and the motivation connects it with the Day of Yahweh which is characterized as destruction from Yahweh. Then comes the description of the problem at hand: there is no food, a fact which is associated with the temple as the source of life and so sustenance. The harvest has been devastated; this in turn affects the cattle, sheep and other beasts because there is no food for them in the pasture. All this is the result of the locust plague. There is a change in v. 19, which begins with the invocation of the divine name and, although in the first person singular, is still concerned with the same crisis, a communal problem.[31] The text goes on to describe further the crisis of the absence of any harvest; even the water is gone. V. 16 clearly puts the section in the context of the community with its use of plural pronouns. Thus these fragments of lament concentrate on the description of the unparalleled crisis at hand.[32] This means that these verses are specifically shaped for the current situation in post-exilic Israel. The unity and prime purpose of the chapter centre in the characterization of this unusual crisis.

In chapter 2 there is a call to alarm and repentance in the midst of this crisis.[33] A sudden change of mood then takes place and the response to the lament follows. There is a clear break in the book at v. 18.[34] From this point on, oracles concerning the future and promising new life and victory for Jerusalem become the point of attention.[35] The material beginning with v. 19 forms a great assurance oracle in response to the preceding lament and is related to the repentance just prior. This is the same pattern found in the community lament psalms in which there is the change from plea to response.[36] The word וַיַּעַן beginning v. 19 shows the oracular nature of the response which is then introduced with the particle הִנְנִי. In vv. 21, 22 the phrase 'Fear not!' is reminiscent of Begrich's reconstruction of the priestly *Heilsorakel*. The material has a hymnic style to it, calling the people to praise and describing the future promise of Yahweh. This is not one simple oracle but is a composite, developed for its setting in Joel.[37]

The response to the people harks back to the laments in chapter 1 of Joel. In the midst of this harvest failure and lack of fertility, v. 20 describes the defeat of the enemy (locusts) who brought about the crisis.[38] Vv. 21-24 respond to the lament in 1.16-20. Fertility is restored with rain as the people are once again in right relationship with Yahweh.[39] Restitution is also promised for the damage caused by the locust plague (v. 25). Yahweh is the one doing this and he is praised for it. Even greater fertility is promised with the beginning of chapter 3 and it is connected with the Day of Yahweh toward which the preceding lament and response lead.[40] It is thus clear that this part of the book of Joel is a response to previous lament and is in the tradition of the oracles in the community laments and the whole phenomenon of the expressions of certainty in the lament psalms.[41]

The book finishes with further oracles about the joy and wonder of the Day of Yahweh and is dependent upon traditional elements, especially Zion and Enthronement Psalms.[42]

What conclusions are we to draw from this material? It is clear that there is a relationship between this prophetic book and the Psalms, especially lament psalms, but does this make Joel a cult prophet? Wolff is not wide of the mark:[43]

> The content of the message to be transmitted is articulated in the form of a great 'lamentation liturgy'. Its component parts constitute a manual, accommodating everything deemed worthy of notice and promulgation. Yet there is no mistaking the distance between the liturgy as here presented and the actual performance of a lament ceremony. This is made especially apparent by the narrative statements in 1:4 and 2:18 which recount the essential facts concerning not only the terrible current catastrophe but also the subsequent renewal of Yahweh's compassion. Each of these brief reports is then elaborated in a most vivid, superbly artistic fashion in the section of liturgical material which follows it. The two liturgical sections exhibit the typical, primary elements of the

conventional lament ceremony; first, the 'call to communal lamentation', expanded into four strophes (1:5-14), followed by cries of lament (1:15-18) and prayers of lament (1:19-20); and second, the closely associated 'assurance oracles answering a plea' with their characteristic features (2:19-27). These major structural parts of a conventional lamentation liturgy have undergone extensive elaboration, and it is only because of the additional content that the liturgy itself becomes worthy of transmission to later generations.

The lament liturgy has been adapted to fit the context of Joel's book—a crisis of harvest failure which is seen as a harbinger of the Day of Yahweh. Traditional psalmic material is applied to this context after the exile. Thus it does not appear that Joel is functioning within the cult. That is the original place of many of the forms and literary pieces he uses, but he has applied them to his own particular historical setting.[44]

In both Joel and Habakkuk, we have seen material which is cultic in origin and which has the same general prophetic function as the expressions of certainty in the lament psalms. However, the forms have been adapted to the prophet's context in order to make the point of the prophecy in its setting. This means that the context of the prophetic function has changed from a liturgical one to a historical one. Habakkuk and Joel are not cult prophets; they use material with a cultic origin but in a different context, as can be seen from the shift in the forms used. Habakkuk and Joel come from specific communal crises rather than liturgical contexts. Once again the function of a text and the context of that function are at the heart of the matter.

Chapter Five

CONCLUSION

The primary focus of the foregoing study is prophetic elements in psalms of lamentation. In order to clarify this focus, it was necessary to set the stage with a consideration of the *Gattung* of lament and its various parts. We argued that the classifications of individual and community lament are valid on the basis of form and content and provide a better basis for study than more narrow cult-functional categories. In a preliminary consideration of the language of the texts discussed, we noted the general nature of the language which confirms a liturgical setting for these texts but which also presents difficulties in determining the *Gattung* of a psalm as well as its *Sitz im Leben*. In light of this, and the figurative nature of much of the language of the laments, we called for caution in the treatment of such texts.

With this in mind, we moved more directly to the question of prophetic elements in the lament psalms. Of particular interest was the certainty of a hearing in the laments since it has often been associated with the oracular form and prophetic elements in the laments, but has not previously been examined in detail. We examined in their cultic setting both individual and community laments containing the certainty of a hearing. Cult we defined as the organized, established worship of Israel, primarily in the temple.

The individual laments treated came from a variety of cultic settings. Among those treated, we argued for two types of prayers of falsely accused persons—one institutional and legal and the other non-institutional and in response to accusations by way of malicious gossip. We proposed the non-institutional setting for Pss. 28; 31; 57; 64. Ps. 7 was treated as an institutional prayer of a falsely accused person. In addition, Ps. 36 was treated as a prayer for asylum in the sanctuary and Ps. 9-10 in the context of a situation of 'domestic corruption'. Ps. 55 was seen in the more general light of persecution, and Ps. 6 as a prayer by one who is sick. Each of these psalms expresses the certainty of a hearing. This certainty, based on the affirmation that the prayer would be heard, is often put in terms of protection for the worshipper. This was frequently related to the downfall of the enemies involved in the crisis effecting the psalm. In some cases, the protection was solely related to the fall of the enemies. The moving force behind this protection of the worshipper is Yahweh's חסד (Pss. 31.17, 22; 6.5; 36.6-11; 57.4). God's חסד is his messenger to effect deliverance. In spite of the crisis at hand, God's love and relationship with the worshipper do not diminish, but continue. Thus the lament psalm becomes an expression of the renewal of this unchanging love (חסד) in the midst of difficulties.[1]

Such demonstrations of faithfulness are also found in community laments. Pss. 12; 14 (53) are spoken in the context of a completely corrupt society. Pss. 85; 126 come from the context of the Autumn Festival in ancient Israel and plead for a renewal of Yahweh's blessing at the turning of the year. Ps. 60 (108) comes from a background of military strife. The expressions of certainty found in these psalms are quite similar to those found in the individual laments. In each psalm, Yahweh's חסד is renewed for his people. Pss. 12; 85; 126 speak primarily of Yahweh's protection of his people, whether in terms of deliverance or future prosperity. Ps. 14 (53) continues this theme of protection of the nation but adds to it the downfall of the enemies. This latter theme is emphasized in Ps. 60 (108) in which Israel's military enemies are defeated. These expressions of certainty are part of the same phenomenon found in the individual laments. All of the psalms considered function in a liturgical setting and plead with Yahweh for help, which is anticipated with the expression of certainty. Such expressions indicate a renewal, in the midst of crisis, of Yahweh's unchanging love or loyalty to his people.

It has then become clear that the certainty of a hearing is a uniform phenomenon in the laments; we argued that it has a prophetic function and affects the psalms in consequence of this. The function of the expressions of certainty is to anticipate future salvation for the worshipper(s). We defined 'prophetic' as essentially predictive and seeking repentance from God's people. The repentance sought in these psalms is from the doubt and despair associated with the crisis at hand, since divine action is not evident. The expressions of certainty in the individual laments are not unrelated to the oracular form, which is usually associated with prophecy, but this relationship is more clearly seen in the community texts, as also is some indication of a 'prophetic experience' leading to the response to the lament. So we have a relatively uniform phenomenon of the certainty of a hearing in the lament psalms, displaying a prophetic purpose but still functioning clearly in a liturgical context. It is important to note again that this does not prejudice what cultic functionary might have responded to the lament with some divine word, if there was any. This could have been executed by a priest as well as the supposed cult prophet.

We also looked briefly at the various explanations given for the presence of these expressions of certainty in the laments. These ranged from seeing the expressions of certainty as additions to the psalms to seeing them as the fruition of the ritual or recital of Israel's *Heilsgeschichte* to the psychological explanation. However, the most promising explanation is that associated with Begrich and the oracle of salvation. An oracle is delivered indicating hope for the worshipper who responds with the expression of certainty. This anticipates and assures deliverance for the worshipper. It also connects the certainty of a hearing further with a form often found in prophetic literature.

We then looked at some implications of our work for psalmic passages in the Prophets. The books of Habakkuk and Joel have often been tied to the cult, especially in terms of cult prophecy. These books clearly exhibit a relationship to the Psalms. The lament form is particularly evident as is the response to lament in terms of Yahweh's unchanging love being experienced anew by his people. There is much psalmic material in these two books but it is also clear that the context in which the material functions has changed. In both cases, the lament form and element of certainty have been adjusted for application to a historical context. The oracular form and experience of the prophet are emphasized along with the theme of repentance. It is clear from vocabulary, form and function that these texts come from a cultic tradition but the context of the prophetic function has shifted from liturgy to history and thus Habakkuk and Joel are not deemed to be cult prophets.

As we proceed to draw conclusions concerning the relationship between psalmody and prophecy, based on our study of lament texts, it is clear that we need to address the issue of methodology. We began our investigation with an attempt to put this issue in historical perspective. Following Gunkel much of the discussion has centred on form and content and what conclusions can be drawn from similarities in these areas. The predominant conclusion can be traced back to

Mowinckel and postulates cult prophets. Prophetic material in the Psalms is to be accounted for by the presence of cult prophets, and cultic material in the Prophets has the same origin or at least betrays influence from it. Aubrey Johnson has expanded this hypothesis in terms of the function of such cult prophets. These are essentially the lines along which the debate has progressed through the work of Würthwein, Jeremias, Quell, and others.

There is clearly a relationship between psalmody and prophecy. A number of prophetic elements have been identified in the Psalter and we have emphasized the certainty of a hearing as one of these. It is also clear that the canonical prophets are not simply opposed to the cult, and use forms originally connected with the cult. However, there is much which is still unknown. The history of prophecy in Israel is still somewhat obscure; thus we have seriously questioned whether we can assuredly speak of cult prophecy in Israel. There is a further form-critical issue involved. Because oracular forms are found in the Psalter, does that necessarily involve a prophet? On the other side, because originally cultic forms are found in the Prophets, does that mean they are still bound to the cult? We have answered these questions in the negative.

Our study concentrated on lament psalms as a fruitful area for research on this topic. Our procedure was to look at the form, content and context of texts, and we sought to move the discussion more in the direction of the context in which a form functions rather than the place of its origin. This procedure has the advantage of avoiding the entangled discussion of cultic functionaries and of looking at meaning in present context rather than a reconstructed original context. This approach has taken us back to the form-critical methodology of Gunkel in which we concentrate on form and function, and is also related to Aubrey Johnson's work in that an important consideration in determining prophetic elements in lament psalms is the function of a passage. We differ from Johnson in his notion of cult prophecy and in questioning the helpfulness of that approach. We identified the expressions of certainty in the lament psalms as a prophetic element in terms of function, and then moved to the question of the context of that function, clearly cultic in the Psalms but with more of a historical setting in Habakkuk and Joel. This approach pushes the study of the relationship between psalmody and prophecy in a different direction from the dominant approach of cult prophecy. It emphasizes the function of texts and the context of that function—whether cult or a particular historical setting.

In other words, there are clearly significant relationships between psalmody and prophecy in terms of form, vocabulary and function.[2] However it is also true that there is at least one important distinction and that is the context in which the texts function. This can be seen in the shifts of form and even of language from psalm to prophetic passage. Psalmody, because of its liturgical context, uses language which is ambiguous enough to cause difficulty in determining its specific *Sitz im Leben*. This is not so true of prophecy. Thus the primary distinction between psalmody and prophecy which we have discerned is the context in which the lament tradition is used. This is a somewhat different direction than those studies which depend on a particular reconstruction of Israel's cult and suggests that comparative studies of form, vocabulary, function and the context in which a text functioned are of central importance.

In no sense do these conclusions resolve all the issues at hand. The relationship between Israel's cult and history is an area that needs further study as does the role of the cult in preserving Old Testament traditions.[3] Our study is not an end in itself but purposes to provide another beginning and direction in the study of Psalmody and Prophecy.

Notes to Introduction

1. Cf. *Die Psalmen*, 1899, and the helpful account of the early literature in R.E. Clements' chapters on the Prophets and the Psalms, *A Century of Old Testament Study*, 1976.

2. Hermann Gunkel, *The Psalms*, 1967; cf. Werner Klatt, *Hermann Gunkel*, 1969.

3. Especially pp. 329ff., 'The Prophetic in the Psalms'. This volume was actually completed by Gunkel's pupil Begrich after Gunkel's death and was published in 1933 though some of it had appeared earlier. Cf. pp. 5*-6* of the *Einleitung* on Begrich's contribution to the volume, which was considerable. Hereafter this work will be noted as Gunkel—Begrich.

4. Sigmund Mowinckel, *Psalmenstudien* III, 'Kultprophetie und prophetische Psalmen', 1923.

5. We accept the view that the psalms treated herein are actual cultic literature but also see the need to apply the form-critical method of classifying and comparing before moving too far into the area of the psalms' cultic function. Cf. Claus Westermann, 'Struktur und Geschichte der Klage im Alten Testament', *ZAW* 66, 1954, p. 45; Mowinckel, *The Psalms in Israel's Worship* I, pp. 23-35.

6. Cf. Mowinckel, *Psalmenstudien* VI, 'Die Psalmdichter', 1924, pp. 48ff.; '"The Spirit" and the "Word" in the Pre-exilic Reforming Prophets', *JBL* 53, 1934, p. 210.

7. Also cf. Mowinckel's later work *The Psalms in Israel's Worship* II, pp. 53ff. This work appeared in 1962 and is a translation of a greatly revised edition of Mowinckel's 1951 volume published in Norwegian under the title *Offersang og Sangoffer*.

8. Cf. Clements, *A Century of Old Testament Study*, pp. 64f., 92ff.

9. W. Robertson Smith, *The Prophets of Israel*, 1895, p. 85.

10. Gustav Hölscher, *Die Profeten*, 1914, p. 143.

11. Cf. Gerhard von Rad, 'Die falschen Propheten', *ZAW* 51, 1933, pp. 109-120; Alfred Jepsen, *Nabi*, 1934; Johannes Pedersen, *Israel* III-IV, 1940, pp. 107ff., and 'The Rôle Played by Inspired Persons Among the Israelites and the Arabs', *Studies in Old Testament Prophecy (Presented to Theodore H. Robinson)*, ed. H.H. Rowley, 1957, pp. 127ff.; Hubert Junker, *Prophet und Seher in Israel*, 1927, pp. 14-41; Johannes Hempel, *Die althebräische Literatur und ihr hellenistisch-jüdisches Nachleben*, 1930, pp. 57, 69; Herbert Gordon May, 'Pattern and Myth in the Old Testament', *JR* 21, 1941, p. 293.

12. *The Cultic Prophet in Ancient Israel*, 1944; cf. Aubrey R. Johnson, 'The

Prophet in Israelite Worship', *ExpT* 47, 1935-36, pp. 312ff.

13. *The Cultic Prophet and Israel's Psalmody*, 1979. Here he assumes the acceptance of his earlier work.

14. *Associations of Cult Prophets Among the Ancient Semites.*

15. Cf. Georg Fohrer, 'Die Propheten des Alten Testaments im Blickfeld neuer Forschung', *BZAW* 99, 1967, pp. 1ff.; Walther Eichrodt, *Theology of the Old Testament* I, 1961, pp. 309ff.; A.H.J. Gunneweg, *Mündliche und schriftliche Tradition der vorexilischen Prophetenbücher*, 1959, pp. 81ff.; J.H. Eaton, *Festal Drama in Deutero-Isaiah*, 1979.

16. Cf. H.-J. Kraus, *Prophetie und Politik*, 1952, pp. 41ff., and *Worship in Israel*, 1966, pp. 101ff.

17. Cf., for example, Abraham J. Heschel, *The Prophets*, 1962, pp. 480ff.; A.S. Herbert, *Worship in Ancient Israel*, 1959, pp. 40ff.; R.B.Y. Scott, *The Relevance of the Prophets*, 1959, p. 43; Th.C. Vriezen, *An Outline of Old Testament Theology*, 1958, pp. 63, 261; Anthony Phillips, 'The Ecstatics' Father', *Words and Meanings: Essays Presented to David Winton Thomas*, ed. Peter R. Ackroyd and Barnabas Lindars, 1968, pp. 192f.; Helmer Ringgren, *Israelite Religion*, 1966, pp. 212ff.; Theophile James Meek, *Hebrew Origins*, 1960, pp. 178ff.; J. Lindblom, *Prophecy in Ancient Israel*, 1973, pp. 206ff.; R.E. Clements, *Prophecy and Covenant*, 1965, pp. 19ff., 86ff. Many of these scholars take the view that there were cult prophets in ancient Israel but that the pre-exilic canonical prophets were not among them.

18. Ernst Würthwein, 'Der Ursprung der prophetischen Gerichtsrede', *ZThK* 49, 1952, pp. 1ff.; it is noteworthy that Würthwein's view can be traced back to Mowinckel's assertion of an ethical element in the cult as part of the background for the ethical demands of the canonical prophets; cf. *Psalmenstudien* III, pp. 41ff. and *The Psalms in Israel's Worship* II, pp. 65ff.

19. 'Kultpolemik oder Kultbescheid? Beobachtungen zu dem Thema "Prophetie und Kult"', *Tradition und Situation, Artur Weiser zum 70. Geburtstag*, ed. Ernst Würthwein and Otto Kaiser, 1963, pp. 115ff.

20. 'Prophetenamt und Mittleramt', *ZThK* 58, 1961, pp. 269ff., and 'Kultisches Recht im Alten Testament', *ZThK* 60, 1963, pp. 297ff., 304.

21. For a more balanced view, cf. H. Gross, 'Gab es in Israel ein "prophetisches Amt"?' *EThL* 41, 1965, pp. 5ff.

22. In order for this to happen, it was necessary that the dichotomy between prophet and priest and between prophet and cult be softened. Such a process was taking place as much of the research on cult prophecy was beginning; cf. the view of Volz, 'Die radikale Ablehnung der Kultreligion durch die alttestamentlichen Propheten', *ZST* 14, 1937, pp. 63ff., and George Buchanan Gray, *Sacrifice in the Old Testament*, 1925, pp. 43-45; John Skinner, *Prophecy and Religion*, 1930, pp. 181ff.; Adolphe Lods, *The Prophets and the Rise of Judaism*, 1937, pp. 68f.; Richard Hentschke, *Die Stellung der vorexilischen Schriftpropheten zum Kultus*, 1957, with W.O.E. Oesterley, *Sacrifices in Ancient Israel*, 1937, pp. 191ff.; Adam C. Welch,

Prophet and Priest in Old Israel, 1936; H.H. Rowley, 'Ritual and the Hebrew Prophets', *From Moses to Qumran*, 1963, pp. 117f., 120, 130f., 134; Rolf Rendtorff, 'Priesterliche Kulttheologie und prophetische Kultpolemik', *ThLZ* 81, 1956, col. 342; Sidney Jellicoe, 'The Prophets and the Cultus', *ExpT* 60, 1948-1949, p. 258; N.W. Porteous, 'Prophet and Priest in Israel', *ExpT* 62, 1950-1951, pp. 4ff.; Otto Plöger, 'Priester und Prophet', *ZAW* 63, 1951, pp. 157ff.; Gunneweg, *Mündliche und schriftliche Tradition der vorexilischen Prophetenbücher*, pp. 84ff.

23. E. von Waldow, *Der traditionsgeschichtliche Hintergrund der prophetischen Gerichtsreden*, 1963, p. 41; Hesse, 'Wurzelt die prophetische Gerichtsrede im israelitischen Kult?' *ZAW* 65, 1953, pp. 45ff.

24. Cf. also Gerhard von Rad, *Old Testament Theology* I, 1962, p. 97; II, 1965, pp. 50ff.; Martin Noth, 'Amt und Berufung im Alten Testament', *Gesammelte Studien zum Alten Testament*, 3rd ed., 1966, pp. 329-331; H.W. Hertzberg, 'Sind die Propheten Fürbitter?' *Tradition und Situation*, pp. 63ff.; they understand the prophets to be basically charismatic rather than part of an institution.

25. 'Der Kultprophet', *ThLZ* 81, 1956, cols. 401ff.

26. *Ancient Israel*, 1961, pp. 384ff.

27. Cf. mainly *Worship in Ancient Israel*, 1967, pp. 144ff.

28. H.H. Rowley, *From Moses to Qumran*, pp. 130, 132-134.

29. Cf. *ibid.*, pp. 126-128; H.H. Rowley, 'The Nature of Old Testament Prophecy in the Light of Recent Study', *The Servant of the Lord*, 1952, p. 112.

30. *The Servant of the Lord*, p. 111.

31. Cf. Rolf Rendtorff, 'נביא in the Old Testament', *TDNT* VI, 1968, pp. 796ff.; von Rad, *Old Testament Theology* II, pp. 51ff.; Hentschke, *Die Stellung der vorexilischen Schriftpropheten*; Menahem Haran, 'From Early to Classical Prophecy: Continuity and Change', *VT* 27, 1977, pp. 385ff.

32. *Kultprophetie und Gerichtsverkündigung in der späten Königszeit Israels*, 1970.

33. Many terms have been used to describe various kinds of prophets. This has often been more confusing than helpful, such as the misleading term 'writing prophets' or the arbitrary distinction between prophets of weal and woe. Unfortunately von Rad's earlier article on false prophets, *ZAW* 51, 1933, pp. 109-120, contributed to the terminological difficulties.

34. As, for example, in H. Schmidt's *Das Gebet der Angeklagten im Alten Testament*, 1928; A.R. Johnson's *Sacral Kingship in Ancient Israel*, 2nd ed., 1967; or Klaus Seybold's *Das Gebet den Kranken im Alten Testament*, 1973.

35. This distinction can be seen in the attempts by recent Psalm commentators such as Weiser or Kraus to put psalms into a cultic setting while interpreters of the Book of Isaiah, for example, seek a historical *Sitz im Leben* for the prophet's work, as R.B.Y. Scott, 'The Book of Isaiah', *IB* V, 1956, pp. 161f. or Brevard S. Childs, *Isaiah and the Assyrian Crisis*, 1967.

36. It is noteworthy that much of the 'psalmic material' in the prophetic books is related to the psalms of lamentation.

Notes to Chapter One

1. There needs to be flexibility in the never-ending investigation of which psalms are included in a particular *Gattung* as well as the relationships between *Gattungen*. Concepts frequently cross the boundaries. A great deal of structural variety is found in the laments; cf. Gunkel—Begrich, pp. 239ff. Methodologically it is important to do the *Gattungen* analysis before moving too far in cult-functional studies in order to ensure that enough comparison has been done; cf. Westermann, *ZAW*, 1954, p. 45; Mowinckel, *The Psalms in Israel's Worship* I, pp. 23-35; though most of the psalms did likely originate in Israel's festivals; cf. A.A. Anderson, *The Book of Psalms* I, 1972, p. 31.

2. Cf. J. Hempel, 'Psalms, Book of', *IDB* III, 1962, p. 950; Gunkel—Begrich, p. 212.

3. Cf. Gunkel—Begrich, pp. 212f. No attempt is made to be exhaustive in the lists of examples cited in this part of the study; all biblical references in this chapter are from the Psalms.

4. Bentzen even notes what he calls a 'primitive cell', probably in the cultic proclamation הנני יהוה; cf. his *Introduction to the Old Testament* I, 1967, p. 156; Georg Fohrer, *Introduction to the Old Testament*, 1970, p. 266.

5. Thus, there is some justification in calling this section an introduction with its various parts as Kraus does in his commentary, I, p. XLV.

6. Cf. Westermann, *The Praise of God in the Psalms*, 1965, p. 34; Gunkel—Begrich, p. 215.

7. There have been many attempts to delineate fully the situation of the speaker in the individual laments. Material, physical, mental, and spiritual suffering may be involved. Sickness is often pointed to as the most common crisis; cf. Gunkel—Begrich, p. 193; Mowinckel, *Psalmenstudien* I, "Åwän und die individuellen Klagepsalmen', 1921 and *The Psalms in Israel's Worship* II, pp. 1ff., but because of the general nature of the language in the psalms, it is difficult to be that specific in every instance. It is probably best to say that the worshipper seeks deliverance from his sojourn in Sheol rather than attempting to be more specific concerning the whole class of psalms; cf. Gunkel—Begrich, pp. 185ff., 190, 195; Christoph Barth, *Die Errettung vom Tode in den individuellen Klage- und Dankliedern des Alten Testaments*, 1947. Sometimes the situation of the community laments is easier to discern but even then the vague language can be a problem.

8. Gunkel—Begrich, p. 218; cf. Westermann, 'The Role of the Lament in the Theology of the Old Testament', *Interpretation* 28, 1974, pp. 26, 32 and

The Praise of God, p. 34. The term 'lamentation' has been retained here because of its widespread acceptance and the essential fact that it is the occasion behind the lament proper which gives rise to the prayer. Thus lament and petition should not be separated but seen as part of the whole psalm of lamentation.

9. Again because of the nature of the language of the psalms, it is quite difficult to be specific about the identification of the enemies in the individual laments as a class. No one explanation will fit all the psalms. Sometimes in the community laments the enemies may be identified more explicitly but even there it is often a problem. Many suggestions have been made as to who the enemies are; cf., for example, Westermann, *ZAW*, pp. 61ff.; Gunkel–Begrich, pp. 196-198, 206ff., 211, 219; Mowinckel, *Psalmenstudien* I and *The Psalms in Israel's Worship*, especially I, pp. 225ff.; Birkeland, *The Evildoers in the Book of Psalms*, 1955; J.H. Eaton, *Kingship and the Psalms*, 1976; George W. Anderson, 'Enemies and Evildoers in the Book of Psalms', *BJRL* 48, 1965/1966, pp. 18-29.

10. Cf. Gunkel–Begrich, p. 235.

11. Gunkel–Begrich, p. 244.

12. Cf. *ibid.*, p. 248; Westermann, *The Praise of God*, pp. 75ff. The vow is clearly an expression of thankgiving, in contrast to Babylonian psalms; cf. Gunkel–Begrich, pp. 247f.; Westermann, *The Praise of God*, pp. 36ff. but also Balla, *Das Ich der Psalmen*, 1912, pp. 86f.

13. Hans Schmidt, *Das Gebet der Angeklagten im Alten Testament* and *Old Testament Essays*, 1927, pp. 143-155; Walter Beyerlin, *Die Rettung der Bedrängten in den Feindpsalmen der Einzelnen auf institutionelle Zusammenhänge untersucht*, 1970, especially pp. 154ff.; cf. L. Delekat, *Asylie und Schutzorakel am Zionheiligtum*, 1967.

14. Mowinckel, *Psalmenstudien* I and *The Psalms in Israel's Worship* II, pp. 1ff.; Klaus Seybold, *Das Gebet den Kranken im Alten Testament*.

15. For example, Mowinckel, *The Psalms in Israel's Worship* I, pp. 30f. and II, p. 8; Beyerlin, *Die Rettung der Bedrängten*, p.158; cf. Matitiahu Tsevat, *A Study of the Language of the Biblical Psalms*, 1955, pp. 35ff.

16. Gunkel–Begrich, p. 189; cf. Hermann Gunkel, 'The Religion of the Psalms', *What Remains of the Old Testament and Other Essays*, 1928, p. 98; Helmer Ringgren, *The Faith of the Psalmists*, 1963, pp. 61f.

17. Cf. Robert C. Culley, *Oral Formulaic Language in the Biblical Psalms*, 1967; William R. Watters, *Formula Criticism and the Poetry of the Old Testament*, 1976.

18. *The Psalms in Israel's Worship* I, pp. 30-31 and II, pp. 1, 8.

19. Gunkel–Begrich, pp. 184, 189f.

20. Cf. Geo Widengren, *The Accadian and Hebrew Psalms of Lamentation*, 1937; Friedrich Stummer, *Sumerisch-akkadische Parallelen zum Aufbau alttestamentlicher Psalmen*, 1922, p. 68, for example.

21. Cf. Becker, *Wege der Psalmenexegese*, 1975, pp. 85ff.

22. Cf. Mowinckel, *The Psalms in Israel's Worship* II, pp. 9f. Delekat also assumes the literalness of the cultic language of laments in identifying the crisis occasioning a particular psalm. For example, he speaks of the financial crises in the first part of Ps. 31 and the last part of Ps. 27 or the suspicion of robbery in Ps. 56. Cf. his treatment of these psalms in *Asylie und Schutzorakel*. His extreme views clearly take this understanding of the language far beyond any possible credibility.

23. Cf. Christoph Barth, *Introduction to the Psalms*, 1966, pp. 43-55, and *Die Errettung vom Tode*.

24. Cf. Gunkel—Begrich, pp. 195, 254; Becker, *Wege der Psalmenexegese*, p. 15. Gunkel's occasional support of this view may be connected with his autobiographical understanding of the laments.

25. Cf. Ernst Cassirer, *Language and Myth*, 1946, pp. 83ff.

Notes to Excursus I

1. 'Ueber das Ich der Psalmen', *ZAW* 8, 1888, pp. 49-147; cf. Clements, *A Century of Old Testament Study*, pp. 76ff.

2. *Das Ich der Psalmen*, 1912; cf. Clements, *A Century of Old Testament Study*, pp. 81, 90. Smend's proposal is not without value since it begins to lead the way toward finding the psalms' *Sitz im Leben* in the nation's cult; it simply does not go far enough.

3. *The Psalms in Israel's Worship*.

4. Harris Birkeland, *The Evildoers in the Book of Psalms*.

5. *Ibid.*, pp. 16ff.; note also his method of *Gattungen* analysis here. Birkeland requires a great deal from the stereotypical language of the psalms in specifying the identity of the enemies which may change from situation to situation. He also apparently takes the view that the basic meaning of a word never changes despite different contexts and times of usage; cf. pp. 13ff.

6. Cf. George W. Anderson, *BJRL*, 1965/1966, p. 20.

7. Despite the impression we might get from Eaton's *Kingship and the Psalms*, pp. 11ff.; cf. Mowinckel, *The Psalms in Israel's Worship* II, pp. 1ff., 255.

8. Cf. Mowinckel, *Psalmenstudien* I.

9. *The Psalms in Israel's Worship* I, pp. 42ff., 225ff.

10. *Kingship and the Psalms*; cf. also his *Psalms*, 1967.

11. Eaton, *Kingship and the Psalms*, pp. 20ff.

12. For example, psalms of the falsely accused from Schmidt and Beyerlin; or asylum from Delekat; or prayers of the sick from Mowinckel and Seybold. Another problem at this point is the ambiguity of the language in the texts which must be the basis for determining *Sitzen im Leben*. This may inhibit the possibility of placing all the psalms in an assured setting.

13. In connection with the royal interpretation, one should also consult Aubrey R. Johnson, *Sacral Kingship in Ancient Israel*, and Aage Bentzen, *King and Messiah*, 1955, where possible reconstructions of a royal ritual in ancient Israel are discussed in relation to the Psalms.

Notes to Chapter Two

1. *Das Gebet der Angeklagten*.
2. *Die Rettung der Bedrängten*.
3. Some commentators who have accepted the metaphorical interpretation have occasionally come close to suggesting the setting proposed herein when they understand the lamenter to be persecuted by slanderers, for example, W.O.E. Oesterley, *The Psalms*, 1953, p. 307; Edward J. Kissane, *The Book of Psalms* I, 1953, p. 271; A.F. Kirkpatrick (ed.), *The Book of Psalms*, 1902, pp. 357, 792. They have not, however, seen the full significance of the worshipper's situation.
4. On the concept of shame, cf. S.J. De Vries, 'Shame', *IDB* IV, pp. 305f.; Johs. Pedersen, *Israel* I-II, 1926, pp. 239ff.; Barth, *Die Errettung vom Tode*, p. 107.
5. Martin A. Klopfenstein, *Scham und Schande nach dem Alten Testament*, 1972, notes both the serious consequences of shame and the nature of the concept in terms of social relationship. Cf. F. Stolz, 'בוש', *THAT* I, 1971, cols. 269ff.; Horst Seebass, 'בוש', *TDOT* II, 1975, pp. 50ff.
6. Cf. William McKane, *Proverbs*, 1970, p. 429.
7. *Exodus*, 1974, p. 425.
8. Isaiah also condemns things which are not forbidden in Israel's law such as pride and drunkenness; cf. Is. 5.11-12, 21-22; 28.1-4; and condemns officials who are writing laws that oppress the helpless; cf. Is. 10.1, 2.
9. Cf. Ze'ev W. Falk, *Hebrew Law in Biblical Times*, 1964, pp. 60, 61, 65-66.
10. Near Eastern parallels can be found in G.R. Driver and John C. Miles, *The Assyrian Laws*, 1935; Cyrus H. Gordon, 'Biblical Customs and the Nuzu Tablets', *BA* III, 1940, pp. 1-12; Julian Morgenstern, 'Trial by Ordeal Among the Semites and in Ancient Israel', *Hebrew Union College Jubilee Volume*, 1925, pp. 113-143; also cf. P. Kyle McCarter, 'The River Ordeal in Israelite Literature', *HTR* 66, 1973, pp. 403-412.
11. G. Henton Davies, *Exodus*, 1967, p. 181.
12. Thus Eaton's rather circular argument for the royal character of Ps. 31 becomes unnecessary, *Kingship and the Psalms*, pp. 67ff.
13. The Masoretic text is retained here to indicate contrast though there is versional and manuscript support for reading the verb in the second person; cf. *BHS*.

14. Perhaps a contemporary paraphrase would be, 'you have set my feet at liberty'.

15. נפשׁי here indicates the very being or self of the worshipper; this is difficult to translate into English.

16. Reading מָאֵר rather than the very awkward meaning derived from the Masoretic pointing; cf. G.R. Driver, 'Studies in the Vocabulary of the Old Testament. II', *JTS* 32, 1931, p. 256; *NEB*.

17. This word is not intended to carry a legal connotation but to indicate the malicious whispering of accusations as gossip.

18. In opposition to Kraus, *Psalmen* I, p. 247.

19. In opposition to Delekat, *Asylie und Schutzorakel*, pp. 101f., 219f. and Hans Schmidt, *Das Gebet der Angeklagten*, p. 10; following A.A. Anderson, *Psalms* I, p. 246; Hermann Gunkel, *Die Psalmen*, 1926, p. 131, and others.

20. Cf. Kraus, *Psalmen* I, p. 248 and Delekat, *Asylie und Schutzorakel*, pp. 219ff. (on vv. 10ff.).

21. Gunkel, *Die Psalmen*, p. 131; Hans Schmidt, *Das Gebet der Angeklagten*, p. 39; cf. Weiser, *The Psalms*, p. 275; Mowinckel, *Psalmenstudien* I, p. 28; Mitchell Dahood, *Psalms* I, 1966, p. 187; Seybold, *Das Gebet den Kranken*, p. 72; Johnson, *Cultic Prophet and Israel's Psalmody*, pp. 302ff.

22. There is little suggestion of a legal setting for the psalm.

23. If one understands the full significance of shame indicated above, Georg Fohrer would appear to be correct, at least for psalms such as Ps. 31, when he says concerning the laments, 'We are instead for the most part dealing with personal enmity of the kind that is not exactly uncommon in everyday life'. *Introduction to the Old Testament*, p. 268.

24. There is little indication of what such a cultic sign might have consisted, though some possibilities have been indicated in the above discussion of means other than judicial ones for obtaining Yahweh's decision in a dispute.

25. Kraus, *Psalmen* I, p. 251; Gunkel, *Die Psalmen*, p. 131.

26. Cf. vv. 8 and 17 and the theme of faithfulness in v. 6 and Johnson, *Cultic Prophet and Israel's Psalmody*, pp. 310f.

27. Cf. Kirkpatrick, *The Book of Psalms*, p. 160. It may also be the case that עיר could be related to a different root (עור —root I, *BDB*, p. 734; III in *K-B*, p. 690) and mean 'agitation' from terror, 'excitement'. Cf. Hans Schmidt, *Das Gebet der Angeklagten*, p. 38.

28. Note also the parallel phrase לבית מצודות.

29. Gunkel, *Die Psalmen*, p. 131; Mowinckel, *Psalmenstudien* I, p. 152 and *The Psalms in Israel's Worship* I, p. 219; cf. Weiser, *The Psalms*, p. 277; Johnson, *Cultic Prophet and Israel's Psalmody*, pp. 310f. Schmidt suggests that the thanksgiving was uttered later after the deliverance, *Das Gebet der Angeklagten*, p. 39; cf. Rudolf Kittel, *Die Psalmen*, 1922, p. 119, where it is claimed that the salvation is assumed in these verses.

30. Cf. Johnson, *Cultic Prophet and Israel's Psalmody*, pp. 302f.

31. Vv. 3f. form a kind of implicit protestation of innocence as a part of the lamenter's plea. Because the evidence is not overwhelming, the placement of Ps. 28 in this setting must be considered tentative though justifiable. There may be little alternative since the language certainly militates against a legal *Sitz im Leben*. The last part of the psalm sounds as though it could refer to the practice of asylum in the sanctuary. Cf. Kraus, *Psalmen* I, p. 229; the view of Gunkel, *Die Psalmen*, p. 120, that the lamenter is sick is unlikely as is that of Kirkpatrick, *The Book of Psalms*, p. 144, that there is pestilence in the land. A.A. Anderson, *Psalms* I, p. 228, relates the psalm to a pilgrimage festival and Delekat, *Asylie und Schutzorakel*, p. 54, places it in an incubation ritual, but it is difficult to be so specific.

32. The מן here indicates that the thanksgiving comes from the song.

33. Reading לעמו with versional and manuscript support; cf. *BHS*. The move to the MT from the text reflected in the Septuagint, Syriac and some Hebrew manuscripts is a simple one, especially with the heavy accent. לעמו fits the context and parallelism more clearly. Note also the use of עם in v. 9.

34. Eaton, *Kingship and the Psalms*, pp. 40ff.; Mowinckel, *The Psalms in Israel's Worship* I, pp. 74, 220; Johnson, *Cultic Prophet and Israel's Psalmody*, pp. 215ff. He understands the entire psalm to be the work of a cult prophet; cf. pp. 13ff. above.

35. Cf. Kraus, *Psalmen* I, p. 231, and especially A.A. Anderson, *Psalms* I, pp. 227-228.

36. *The Psalms in Israel's Worship* II, p. 11.

37. A.A. Anderson, *Psalms* I, p. 227; cf. W.T. Davison (ed.), *The Psalms* I, n.d., p. 147.

38. Kirkpatrick, *The Book of Psalms*, p. 144, attributes the certainty to faith but cf. p. 146.

39. *The Psalms in Israel's Worship* I, p. 219; cf. Gunkel, *Die Psalmen*, p. 119; Weiser, *The Psalms*, p. 256; and Johnson's helpful comments, *Cultic Prophet and Israel's Psalmody*, pp. 220-222.

40. For example, by Kraus, *Psalmen* I, p. 77; A.A. Anderson, *Psalms* I, p. 104; Gunkel, *Die Psalmen*, pp. 32f.

41. Perhaps the corruptions in the acrostic poem are part of the problem at this point; cf. Weiser, *The Psalms*, p. 149.

42. Cf. Gunkel, *Die Psalmen*, pp. 32ff.; Kraus, *Psalmen* I, p. 79; Weiser, *The Psalms*, p. 149.

43. *The Psalms in Israel's Worship* I, p. 95; cf. Beyerlin, 'Die *tôdä* der Heilsvergegenwärtigung in den Klageliedern des Einzelnen', *ZAW* 79, 1967, pp. 208-224, especially pp. 221ff.

44. *Psalms* I, p. 105. Laments and thanksgivings are often related and it is frequently the vow of praise which links them. Cf. Ps. 7.18 (ending a lament) with Ps. 9.3.

45. The attempt by Kirkpatrick, *The Book of Psalms*, p. 42, to relate these two aspects of the psalm probably cannot be accepted. Citing these aspects of

the text, Eaton, *Kingship and the Psalms*, pp. 32f., regards the psalm as royal; this is unlikely. Cf. Beyerlin, *ZAW*, 1967, pp. 221ff., who shows that the first part of the psalm, the song of thanksgiving, is concerned with the great acts of God in general rather than with the particular circumstances of this worshipper.

46. Cf. A.A. Anderson, *Psalms* I, p. 118.

47. Cf. Robert Gordis, 'Psalm 9-10—a Textual and Exegetical Study', *JQR* 48, 1957-1958, p. 107. Delekat, *Asylie und Schutzorakel*, pp. 104ff., goes entirely too far in delineating the circumstances behind the psalm. Hans Schmidt, *Die Psalmen*, pp. 17f., understands the lamenter to be falsely accused.

48. The text is retained but there may be a problem with תכין; cf. *BHS*; Jacob Leveen, 'A Note on Ps. 10:17-18', *JBL* 67, 1948, pp. 249-250 and 'Psalm X: A Reconstruction', *JTS* 45, 1944, pp. 16ff. It is difficult to accept either of Leveen's proposals on these verses though he is clearly aware of the problems in the text.

49. Literally, 'to give justice to the forsaken and oppressed, not (allowing anyone) yet again to frighten men from the land'. Yahweh's purpose is indicated with the infinitives.

50. Note the use of תאות in 10.3 and 17 referring to opposite groups.

51. It could have the character of testimony as Eaton suggests; cf. *Kingship and the Psalms*, p. 32.

52. The vocabulary of this section is quite similar to that of Ps. 9, again supporting the view that Ps. 9-10 is a unity. For example, אבד occurs (in various forms) in Ps. 10.16 and 9.4, 6, 7, 19; גוים in 10.16 and 9.6, 16, 18, 20, 21; and שפט (in various forms) in 10.18 and 9.5, 9, 20.

53. The term גוים is used here to characterize the enemies in order to relate them to the manifestation of Yahweh's kingship in Ps. 9. The description of them in Ps. 10 does not lend credence to the view that they are foreign oppressors but their activities have a similar result for the oppressed.

54. Gunkel, *Die Psalmen*, pp. 36f.

55. Cf. Kraus, *Psalmen* I, p. 86, on the significance of the term אנוש.

56. *Die Psalmen*, p. 37; cf. Diethelm Michel, *Tempora und Satzstellung in den Psalmen*, 1960, p. 91.

57. *The Book of Psalms*, p. 56.

58. אברו in v. 16 could actually refer to any time frame as the translations of the *RSV* and *NEB* show. The point of the form is that the action is considered accomplished. It could refer back to Ps. 9, supporting the unity of the whole composition, and/or to the worshipper's situation at the end of Ps. 10.

59. Weiser, *The Psalms*, p. 150, relates the change to a theophany in the cult. It is also conceivable that the entire psalm was used after the deliverance as a song of thanksgiving but the lament categorization used above is more likely.

60. Kraus, *Psalmen* I, pp. 402-403; Gunkel, *Die Psalmen*, pp. 237-238. Gunkel relates the first part to a custom of pilgrimage which has now been denied, and places the second part in the diaspora while Kraus relates that part to persecution by Arabian tribes. Cf. Weiser, *The Psalms*, p. 419, who also relates the persecution to fraud and oppression but indicates our inability to recover the specific circumstances behind the psalm. Though the entire poem has a disjointed character, it is considered as a unity here.

61. Mowinckel, *The Psalms in Israel's Worship* I, p. 219; II, p. 20; Eaton, *Kingship and the Psalms*, p. 74; Kirkpatrick, *The Book of Psalms*, p. 308.

62. Cf. Delekat, *Asylie und Schutzorakel*, pp. 181f., who relates the psalm to a trial but also cf. A.A. Anderson, *Psalms*, p. 412.

63. The text is difficult here and the Greek and Latin versions use a passive form but the Masoretic text is understandable; cf. *BHS*.

64. Though the verbal form is not passive, this translation seems best to convey its sense. The verb is also put with v. 4 for reasons of metre and meaning. The Septuagint and Jerome support this.

65. The text is retained here; cf. *BDB*, p. 557.

66. It is clear that one of the enemies is a past friend of the worshipper (vv. 13-15).

67. The sudden occurrence of the perfect פדה is odd but can probably be retained; cf. *G-K*, par. 119gg and *BHS*.

68. The text of v. 20 is unaltered with the exception that סלה is likely misplaced. The meaning of וישב is a problem, however; cf. *RSV*. An exact identification of the region called 'East' is impossible. The literal sense of the last part of the line is 'and he will humble them, that is (the) dweller(s) of (in) the East'.

69. Read בשלמיו for בשלמיו; cf. *K-B*, p. 979.

70. Gunkel sees this first part of the passage as a wish or curse but that is unlikely in this context; *Die Psalmen*, p. 238; cf. also Beyerlin, *Die Rettung der Bedrängten*, p. 24.

71. Cf. Weiser, *The Psalms*, p. 420, who sees this section referring to Yahweh as judge.

72. The conjecture that this reference is to Arabian tribes as in Kraus, *Psalmen* I, p. 405; Gunkel, *Die Psalmen*, pp. 238, 241, is entirely too subjective and so rejected here.

73. Cf. Kirkpatrick, *The Book of Psalms*, p. 313; A.A. Anderson, *Psalms* I, p. 418.

74. Cf. A.A. Anderson, *Psalms* I, p. 418.

75. This is probably the significance of the verb ענה.

76. *Die Psalmen*, p. 238.

77. *Psalmen* I, pp. 402-405; cf. Delekat, *Asylie und Schutzorakel*, p. 185; A.A. Anderson, *Psalms* I, p. 419.

78. A jussive sense (as a final petition) for the verbs would not fit the context.

79. Cf. Eaton, *Kingship and the Psalms*, p. 75.

80. Gunkel is, however, unsure of that possibility, *Die Psalmen*, p. 21; cf. Mowinckel, *Psalmenstudien* I, p. 9; Johnson, *Cultic Prophet and Israel's Psalmody*, pp. 237ff., who understands this psalm to be the work of a cult prophet as described above, pp. 13ff.

81. *Das Gebet den Kranken*, pp. 153-158.

82. Cf. Johnson, *Cultic Prophet and Israel's Psalmody*, p. 240.

83. It is possible that the language of this lament is primarily figurative and intended simply to describe a grave crisis. The place of the enemies in the crisis is unclear here as elsewhere in these laments.

84. Cf. *Psalmenstudien* I; *The Psalms in Israel's Worship* II, pp. 1ff. Of course, prior to Mowinckel's work, Gunkel proposed that sickness was the setting for many individual laments, *Die Psalmen*; Gunkel-Begrich, pp. 190ff.

85. Such a setting would, of course, be common in any society and so it is only natural that their prayer literature would reflect such a crisis. Mowinckel, *The Psalms in Israel's Worship* II, pp. 2ff., and Seybold, *Das Gebet den Kranken*, especially pp. 82ff., also refer to other Old Testament texts supporting such a *Sitz im Leben* for psalms.

86. Cf. Pss. 119.115; 139.19.

87. *Psalmen* I, pp. 50-51; cf. Johnson, *Cultic Prophet and Israel's Psalmody*, pp. 240ff.

88. Franz Delitzsch, *Biblical Commentary on the Psalms* I, 1887, p. 173, says the verb indicates that the hearing has actually happened.

89. C.A. and E.G. Briggs, *The Book of Psalms* I, 1906, p. 51. Gunkel interprets the last verse as a curse on the enemies which is certainly conceivable with the idea of the effectiveness of the spoken word, *Die Psalmen*, p. 22. Note the fact that as requested Yahweh has now turned to the lamenter (שׁוּ, v. 4) and so now the enemies are turned back in defeat (שׁוּב, v. 11).

90. Cf. Ps. 35.4, 26.

91. Cf. Seybold, *Das Gebet den Kranken*, pp. 153ff.

92. *The Psalms in Israel's Worship* II, p. 6.

93. Cf. Ridderbos, *Die Psalmen*, p. 99.

94. Cf. Michel, *Tempora und Satzstellung*, p. 63.

95. Though the independent existence of a 'prophetic perfect' in Hebrew is difficult to support, it is clear that the perfect can refer to the future perceived as accomplished; cf. *G-K*, par. 106a, m, n; A.B. Davidson, *Hebrew Syntax*, 1902, p. 61; S.R. Driver, *A Treatise on the Use of the Tenses in Hebrew*, 1892, p. 20. Contrast G.R. Driver, *Problems of the Hebrew Verbal System*, 1938, p. 135. Perhaps 'perfect of certainty' is an appropriate nomenclature here indicating the speaker's conception of the action; cf. Tryggve N.D. Mettinger, 'The Hebrew Verb System, A Survey of Recent Research', *ASTI* IX, 1974, p. 74; Davidson, *An Introductory Hebrew Grammar*, 1947, p. 72.

96. *Das Gebet den Kranken*, p. 157.

97. So Oesterley, *The Psalms*, p. 136; cf. Delekat, *Asylie und Schutzorakel*, pp. 23, 64-65.

98. So Gunkel, *Die Psalmen*, p. 22; cf. Mowinckel, *Psalmenstudien* I, pp. 149f. and *The Psalms in Israel's Worship* II, p. 11; Weiser, *The Psalms*, p. 133.

99. Kraus, *Psalmen* I, p. 281, relates it to asylum as does Delekat, *Asylie und Schutzorakel*, pp. 239f., though in a different way. Mowinckel, *The Psalms in Israel's Worship* I, pp. 164, 220, sees the text as a protective psalm.

100. Cf. N.M. Nicolsky, 'Das Asylrecht in Israel', *ZAW* 48, 1930, pp. 146ff., on this point and the whole concept of asylum in Israel. Also cf. Moshe Greenberg, 'The Biblical Conception of Asylum', *JBL* 78, 1959, pp. 125ff. Greenberg accepts the view that the Deuteronomic reform secularized the meaning of asylum but suggests that cities may still have been used for this purpose before the reform.

101. Though there is certainly not full agreement on this point, cf., for example, Anthony Phillips, *Deuteronomy*, 1973, p. 130, the practice appears to be an attempt to control the operation of an automatic blood vengeance.

102. Cf. Nicolsky, *ZAW*, 1930, p. 174; Gerhard von Rad, *Deuteronomy*, 1966, p. 128.

103. For example, J. Alberto Soggin, *Joshua*, 1972, p. 198; John Gray (ed.), *Joshua, Judges, Ruth*, 1967, pp. 172f.

104. Beyerlin, *Die Rettung der Bedrängten*, has understood the practice of asylum to be relevant to the Psalms but primarily as a part of the procedure in which he finds the setting for prayers of falsely accused men. The worshipper is allowed to enter the sanctuary in order to plea for a definitive divine judgment. Cf. also Kraus, *Psalmen* I, pp. 281, 433; A.A. Anderson, *Psalms* I, pp. 120, 140; Weiser, *The Psalms*, p. 155.

105. *Asylie und Schutzorakel*. Delekat clearly applies his theory too universally in the Psalms. He also apparently misunderstands the temporary nature of asylum in the Old Testament.

106. This takes the Masoretic text to be articulating the concern of the worshipper in this prayer—the appeal of evil to his enemy—but cf. *BHS*.

107. That is, the enemy calls forth his own perverseness to hate others.

108. Cf. L.A.F. Le Mat, *Textual Criticism and Exegesis of Psalm XXXVI*, 1957, pp. 50ff.

109. The contrast is a literary device which is a significant stylistic part of the psalm rather than an indication of a lack of unity.

110. Cf. Ronald E. Clements, 'Temple and Land: A Significant Aspect of Israel's Worship', *TGUOS* 19, 1963, pp. 16ff., for the indication of possible further significance in the act of entering the temple, in this case for asylum.

111. Note the use of חסד and צדקה; cf. vv. 6f.

112. Note the use of רשע in vv. 2 and 12.

113. The introductory particle שם can be used poetically to point to a spot

in which a scene is localized vividly in the imagination, *BDB*, p. 1027; cf. Briggs, *The Book of Psalms* I, p. 332; B.D. Eerdmans, *The Hebrew Book of Psalms*, 1947, p. 220; Weiser, *The Psalms*, pp. 306, 312, who relates the term to a cultic act showing the downfall of the enemies. Also cf. A.A. Anderson, *Psalms* I, p. 291.

114. Cf. the use of אוּן in vv. 4, 5.

115. Gunkel, *Die Psalmen*, p. 153; A.A. Anderson, *Psalms* I, p. 291; Kraus, *Psalmen* I, p. 284.

116. Following Weiser, *The Psalms*, p. 312.

117. *The Book of Psalms*, p. 183; cf. Eaton, *Kingship and the Psalms*, p. 69, who understands the verse as an expression of confidence.

118. As Beyerlin claims, but probably not in the way Delekat proposes, *Asylie und Schutzorakel*, pp. 60ff.; also in opposition to the view of Eaton, *Kingship and the Psalms*, pp. 30ff., and Mowinckel, *The Psalms in Israel's Worship* I, pp. 207, 226. It must also be said that the attempt of Schmidt to be more specific about the crime with which the lamenter is charged is unjustified, *Das Gebet der Angeklagten*, pp. 17-18; cf. Weiser, *The Psalms*, p. 135.

119. *Das Gebet der Angeklagten*; cf. *Die Psalmen*, 1934, and above, pp. 32ff.; also Gunkel—Begrich, pp. 253f.

120. One of the problems with Beyerlin's reconstruction of this cultic setting is that the detail he includes goes beyond the available evidence.

121. Cf. von Rad, *Deuteronomy*, p. 118.

122. This is the pausal form of the plural abstract noun חיים with first common singular suffix.

123. Cf. *K-B*, p. 262, on v. 12b; Beyerlin, *Die Rettung der Bedrängten*, pp. 95ff.; Pss. 9.19; 57.6; von Rad, *Old Testament Theology* I, pp. 357ff.

124. Reading עוּרה אלי with versional support; cf. *BHS*. This follows the Septuagint and fits this section of the psalm which is directed to Yahweh; cf. the beginning of v. 7. Cf. A.A. Anderson, *Psalms* I, p. 96.

125. *K-B*, p. 262. The sense is of denouncing the wicked with indignation since God's imprecation will be accomplished.

126. The enemy is probably the subject of this section rather than God. Then no change of subject is required for v. 15. A change of subject at v. 13 is more likely since vv. 7-12 are in the traditional style of a judgment doxology which the worshipper uses in his plea for justice.

127. These verbs in the perfect tense are translated in the English past tense though they could be rendered with a present since they are describing the enemies and their actions. The past seems to fit the context better here. The translation of the parallel verbs is also a problem. ויהפרהו may indicate the clearing out of the pit; cf. *NEB*.

128. This is accurate unless one understands the first part of v. 14 to express the same concept found in vv. 16f., 'He has prepared deadly weapons *for himself*'. This is most unlikely. Cf. Gunkel, *Die Psalmen*, p. 24.

129. For example, animals, v. 3, in opposition to Weiser, *The Psalms*, p. 136, and Nicolaj Nicolsky, *Spuren magischer Formeln in den Psalmen*, 1927, pp. 93f.; warriors, vv. 13f.; and giving birth to lies, v. 15.

130. Going down to Sheol may be a part of the figure here but it is not the primary concept involved.

131. *Die Psalmen*, p. 27; Gunkel also finds a word-play in ויפל and יפעל. The origin of this concept should perhaps be related to the *lex talionis* (cf. Ex. 21.23ff.; Deut. 19.18ff.) or the wisdom traditions (cf. Prov. 26.27; Ecc. 10.8). Cf. A.A. Anderson, *Psalms* I, p. 428.

132. *The Psalms*, p. 139.

133. Cf. Pss. 9.16; 31.5; 57.7; J.A. Soggin, 'שוב', *THAT* II, 1976, cols. 884ff.

134. *The Book of Psalms* I, p. 60.

135. *Das Gebet der Angeklagten*, p. 19.

136. Cf. Mowinckel, *The Psalms in Israel's Worship* I, p. 220; Weiser, *The Psalms*, p. 426; Eaton, *Kingship and the Psalms*, p. 46, who in a programmatic way understands Ps. 57 to be a royal psalm.

137. *Das Gebet der Angeklagten*, p. 22; cf. Gunkel, *Die Psalmen*, p. 246.

138. *Psalmen* I, p. 412.

139. *Die Rettung der Bedrängten*, pp. 129f.

140. A.A. Anderson, *Psalms* I, p. 427. The 'lying down' in v. 5 is to be understood in this way rather than as referring to an incubation rite.

141. Delekat favours asylum as the setting of the psalm but in an odd way, *Asylie und Schutzorakel*, pp. 213f.

142. The sense of the text seems to be that God is effective in his work on behalf of the worshipper.

143. Though the participle is singular, the plural is used to indicate the collective group of enemies later described in the psalm. This is reflected in the Septuagint and Syriac.

144. Kraus, *Psalmen* I, p. 413, understands it as a petition; Gunkel, *Die Psalmen*, p. 246, as a wish, but cf. Kirkpatrick, *The Book of Psalms*, p. 322.

145. This verb may also be derived from another root meaning 'to frustrate, disappoint, confuse'. Cf. G.R. Driver, 'Studies in the Vocabulary of the Old Testament. IV', *JTS* 33, 1932, pp. 38ff.; *K-B*, pp. 335-336. One wonders if this meaning is strong enough for the present context. Cf. also S.R. Driver, *Tenses in Hebrew*, p. 206, for another possible translation.

146. Beyerlin, *Die Rettung der Bedrängten*, p. 134, notes that חסד and אמת are responsible for the worshipper's deliverance.

147. For a parallel, cf. D. Winton Thomas (ed.), *Documents from Old Testament Times*, 1958, p. 274; cf. A.A. Anderson, *Psalms* I, p. 428, who points out that this refers to God's action on behalf of the poet; and Pss. 7.16f.; 9.16.

148. Cf. Gunkel, *Die Psalmen*, p. 246.

149. Dahood, *Psalms* II, 1968, pp. 53f., understands נפלו in this verse as a precative perfect. The existence of a precative perfect is rejected here as an

imposition on Hebrew from other Semitic languages which has not been substantiated from the Old Testament. Cf. *G-K*, par. 106n, footnote 2; but cf. par. 112aa, on the perfect with consecutive; S.R. Driver, *Tenses in Hebrew*, p. 25; especially note his comment on Arabic parallels. Contrast Davidson, *Hebrew Syntax*, p. 63; G.R. Driver, *Problems of the Hebrew Verbal System*, p. 117. The explanation of the verbs given in the treatment of this psalm is far superior to the tortuous procedure of Moses Buttenwieser, *The Psalms*, 1938, pp. 21-24.

150. Cf. Kraus, *Psalmen* I, pp. 413-414; Weiser, *The Psalms*, p. 427.

151. Cf. Kirkpatrick, *The Book of Psalms*, pp. 356ff.; A.A. Anderson, *Psalms* I, p. 461. Mowinckel understands the crisis referred to in this psalm still to be in the future, *The Psalms in Israel's Worship* I, p. 219, while Weiser places the recitation of the psalm after the crisis, *The Psalms*, p. 458.

152. *Psalmen* I, p. 446.

153. *Asylie und Schutzorakel*, pp. 69f.

154. *Die Rettung der Bedrängten*, pp. 29f.; his view is more tentative.

155. Literally, 'tread' as in bending a bow.

156. Reading לנו; cf. *BHS*. This follows the Syriac and Jerome with little change in the text. It is more appropriate to the context of quoting the enemies.

157. Also note the use of דבר in v. 6.

158. Following Beyerlin's tentative view, *Die Rettung der Bedrängten*, pp. 29f.

159. This reflects a change in accents to facilitate meaning.

160. מכותם is translated in the singular as more appropriate for modern English though the plural form evidently refers to the overthrow of all the enemies.

161. לשונם is taken collectively.

162. The suffix attached to כשל is taken to refer loosely to מכותם in v. 8. This seems the best solution to the problem despite the differences in gender and number.

163. Westermann, *The Praise of God*, pp. 71-73, would call the first letter in v. 8 a '*waw*-adversative', which may take the contrasting function of the *waw* too seriously but the conjunction does apparently serve such a purpose here and elsewhere. Cf. Davidson, *Hebrew Grammar*, p. 168 and *Hebrew Syntax*, p. 203. There are also other introductory particles (Pss. 28.6; 31.22; 36.13) which set off new sections. Cf. James Muilenburg, 'The Linguistic and Rhetorical Usages of the Particle כי in the Old Testament', *HUCA* 32, 1961, pp. 135-160.

164. A.A. Anderson, *Psalms* I, p. 463.

165. *The Book of Psalms*, p. 359.

166. Cf. v. 5 (פתאם).

167. Gunkel, *Die Psalmen*, p. 270, sees the verses as beginning with a curse and Kraus, *Psalmen* I, pp. 446f., considers this as well as noting that the

enemies' punishment comes immediately from their guilt.

168. Following Gunkel, *Die Psalmen*, p. 271, and apparently the RSV.

169. Delekat, *Asylie und Schutzorakel*, pp. 69f., understands an oracle to be involved but in an unusual way.

170. Cf. Gunkel, *Die Psalmen*, p. 271; A.A. Anderson, *Psalms* I, p. 460; Kirkpatrick, *The Book of Psalms*, p. 359; Beyerlin, *Die Rettung der Bedrängten*, p. 29. Kraus, *Psalmen* I, p. 446, characterizes the section as a report of God's intervention.

171. This is where the emphasis of the psalms is rather than on the judgment of the wicked, though the two cannot be totally separated. Contrast Beyerlin, *Die Rettung der Bedrängten*, pp. 38ff.

172. Though not assured, there are also other psalms in which this phenomenon probably occurs—Pss. 27; 56; 94; 140.

173. The vague language of the laments is, of course, also found in the expressions of certainty. This kind of general language is also found in prophetic literature. Witness the difficulty of dating many prophetic oracles.

174. Oracular elements in the Psalter could have a priestly origin; cf., for example, Mowinckel, *Psalmenstudien* III, pp. 23, 105ff.; Johnson, *The Cultic Prophet*, pp. 4, 8, 25; Porteous, *ExpT*, 1950-1951, p. 8. This is also true of the certainty of a hearing.

Notes to Chapter Three

1. Cf. Norman H. Snaith, *The Distinctive Ideas of the Old Testament*, 1944 (1964 ed.), p. 100.

2. As Snaith, *Distinctive Ideas*, pp. 94ff.; W.F. Lofthouse, 'Ḥen and Ḥesed in the Old Testament', *ZAW* 51, 1933, pp. 31ff.; cf. Walther Zimmerli, 'חסד', *TDNT* IX, 1974, pp. 382ff.; E.M. Good, 'Love in the Old Testament', *IDB* III, pp. 164ff.; H.J. Stoebe, 'חסד', *THAT* I, cols. 600ff.

3. *BDB*, p. 821.

4. *Die Psalmen*, p. 44.

5. *The Psalms*, p. 158.

6. *The Psalms in Israel's Worship* II, p. 216.

7. This is apparently the meaning of the text: 'I will place (him) in (the) safety; he pants for it', literally. The versions seem to vary from this in the attempt to make sense of this difficult text in its context; cf. *BHS*; Kraus, *Psalmen* I, p. 97.

8. This is an obscure phrase for which many suggestions have been made. The translation given takes עליל to be the instrument used for the purifying being discussed, a furnace dug into the ground; cf. *BDB*, p. 760; K-B, p. 708.

9. *Right and Wrong; An Interpretation of Some Psalms*, 1952, pp. 12, 51f. Cf. Kirkpatrick, *The Book of Psalms*, p. 61.

10. A.A. Anderson, *Psalms* I, p. 126; cf. Mowinckel, *The Psalms in Israel's Worship* I, p. 218 and II, p. 60; Gunkel, *Die Psalmen*, p. 44.

11. Kraus, *Psalmen* I, pp. 96f.

12. Cf. Weiser, *The Psalms*, p. 160.

13. The verse could be translated, 'You, Yahweh, will protect them; you will preserve us from this generation forever'. Perhaps the jussive force is better, however, given the last verse. The change of persons here is not unusual. Cf. A.A. Anderson, *The Psalms* I, p. 127; *G-K*, par. 126g,h; Briggs, *The Book of Psalms* I, p. 99.

14. Mowinckel, *The Psalms in Israel's Worship* I, pp. 191, 223; A.A. Anderson, *Psalms* II, p. 864; Weiser, *The Psalms*, p. 760, 762.

15. *Psalmen*, pp. 854f.

16. *Die Psalmen*, pp. 551f.

17. Following the suggested reading of *BHS*. There is support in the Septuagint and manuscripts; cf. v. 4. The phrase is used several times; cf. Briggs, *The Book of Psalms* I, p. 111; A.A. Anderson, *Psalms* II, p. 864. The derivation of שבות is much debated but relation to שוב is perhaps most convincing; cf. William L. Holladay, *The Root ŠÛBH in the Old Testament*, 1958, pp. 110ff.

18. So Ernst Ludwig Dietrich, שוב שבות *Die Endzeitliche Wiederherstellung bei den Propheten*, 1925, pp. 18f.; Gunkel, *Die Psalmen*, p. 551.

19. Cf. Eberhard Baumann, 'שוב שבות Eine exegetische Untersuchung', *ZAW* 62, 1950, p. 141; Johnson, *The Cultic Prophet*, p. 67; Soggin, *THAT* II, cols. 886ff.

20. A.A. Anderson, *Psalms* II, p. 864.

21. John Strugnell, 'A Note on Ps. CXXVI.I', *JTS*, n.s. 7, 1956, pp. 239ff., translates the last part of the verse, 'then we were as hale men', that is men who had been (were) healed. The text is in order and the translation usually given and which we follow is quite satisfactory when we realize that the preposition כ on כחלמים puts us in a hypothetical situation. This responds to Strugnell's difficulty with the view that Israel is dreaming here. The remainder of the psalm makes clear the reality of Israel's deliverance. Strugnell's translation, while possible, is then not necessary or preferable to the more frequent sense of חלם; cf. *BDB*, p. 321. The context of great joy also supports this view. Cf. W. Beyerlin, *We are like Dreamers*, Edinburgh, 1982, for whom dreaming combines the reality of both oppression and deliverance.

22. *Die Psalmen*, pp. 551f.

23. Following A.A. Anderson, *Psalms* II, p. 863; Mowinckel, *The Psalms in Israel's Worship* I, p. 223; Kraus, *Psalmen* II, p. 854. Such appeals to past deliverance are common in lament psalms such as Pss. 22; 44; 77; 85; 106.

24. Cf. Baumann, *ZAW*, 1929, p. 22.

25. *Psalmen* II, p. 857.
26. Cf. Ps. 129 and A.A. Anderson, *Psalms* II, p. 866.
27. Gunkel, *Die Psalmen*, p. 552.
28. *The Psalms in Israel's Worship* I, p. 223.
29. *ZAW*, 1950, p. 141; cf. William R. Taylor and W. Stewart McCullough, 'The Book of Psalms', *IB* IV, 1955, p. 666.
30. *The Psalms in Israel's Worship* I, p. 191.
31. A.A. Anderson, *Psalms* II, pp. 607f.; cf. Weiser, *The Psalms*, pp. 579ff.
32. *Die Psalmen*, p. 373.
33. *Psalmen* II, pp. 589ff.; cf. Kirkpatrick, *The Book of Psalms*, p. 510.
34. *Die Psalmen*, p. 373.
35. Cf. Johnson, *Cultic Prophet and Israel's Psalmody*, pp. 200ff.
36. Cf. Baumann, *ZAW*, 1950, pp. 141ff.; A.A. Anderson, *Psalms* II, p. 607; Gunkel, *Die Psalmen*, p. 374; Kirkpatrick, *The Book of Psalms*, pp. 511f.; Mowinckel, *The Psalms in Israel's Worship* II, p. 61; Johnson, *Cultic Prophet and Israel's Psalmody*, pp. 199f.
37. Cf. Johnson, *Cultic Prophet and Israel's Psalmody*, pp. 205-207, who notes the possibility of reading כסל but the Masoretic Text is understandable in its present form.
38. A.A. Anderson, *Psalms* II, p. 611.
39. Cf. Kraus, *Psalmen* II, p. 593.
40. Cf. A.A. Anderson, *Psalms* II, p. 612; Gunkel, *Die Psalmen*, p. 374; Weiser, *The Psalms*, p. 574.
41. Cf. *BDB*, p. 375; H.J. Stoebe, 'טוב', *THAT* I, cols. 661ff.
42. *Cultic Prophet and Israel's Psalmody*, pp. 207f.
43. *The Psalms in Israel's Worship* II, p. 63.
44. 'Wisdom Motifs in Psalm 14.53—*nābāl* and *'ēṣāh*', *BASOR* 220, 1975, pp. 15ff.; he also dates the psalm during the monarchical era. Cf. Gunkel, *Die Psalmen*, p. 232f.; A.A. Anderson, *Psalms* I, pp. 130f.
45. *The Psalms*, p. 164.
46. *Die Psalmen*, pp. 232f.
47. Cf. Briggs, *The Book of Psalms* I, p. 110; Bennett, *BASOR*, 1975, p. 19, on the relation of שם to the sanctuary as the place of vindication.
48. This returns us to the rebounding results of the acts of the wicked. The fool (v. 1) has done abominable things which now are done to him. His plight has been reversed.
49. Cf. Buber, *Right and Wrong*, p. 21.
50. Cf. Kraus, *Psalmen* I, pp. 105, 107f.; Weiser, *The Psalms*, p. 166.
51. Gunkel, *Die Psalmen*, p. 233.
52. *Ibid.*
53. Cf. K. Budde, 'Psalm Problems. II. Psalms XIV and LIII', *ExpT* 12, 1900/1901, p. 286.
54. Cf. Kirkpatrick, *The Book of Psalms*, p. 303, and the various attempts to harmonize the texts, for example, Budde, 'Psalm 14 und 53', *JBL* 47,

1928, pp. 160ff. and *ExpT*, 1900/1901, pp. 285ff.; C.C. Torrey, 'The Archetype of Psalms 14 and 53', *JBL* 46, 1927, pp. 186ff.

55. The Greek moves the phrase to the passive indicating that the enemy will be shamed but there is little difference effectively.

56. Budde's interpretation of Ps. 14 (53) is clearly outmoded but his comments on the development of the psalm to its present text are most interesting. At least he was unaware of redaction in the text and how that might have related to its language and function, *ExpT*, 1900/1901, p. 288.

57. A.A. Anderson, *Psalms* I, p. 441.

58. Cf. Johnson, *Cultic Prophet and Israel's Psalmody*, p. 174.

59. The translation here is somewhat difficult. The figure of speech is apparently that the reeling has been given to the people as wine to drink.

60. The translation here is difficult; cf. Johnson, *Cultic Prophet and Israel's Psalmody*, p. 166.

61. Reading the *Ketib* as the parallelism would suggest.

62. Literally, 'the protection of my head', indicating the function of a helmet.

63. Cf. Johnson, *Cultic Prophet and Israel's Psalmody*, p. 168.

64. Cf. Gunkel, *Die Psalmen*, pp. 256f.

65. Following Gunkel, *Die Psalmen*, pp. 257f.

66. Cf. Baumann, *ZAW*, 1950, p. 120; Gunkel, *Die Psalmen*, pp. 257f.; Eaton, *Kingship and the Psalms*, p. 60.

67. Cf. A.A. Anderson, *Psalms* I, p. 441; Weiser, *The Psalms*, p. 438; Gunkel, *Die Psalmen*, p. 258.

68. *Cultic Prophet and Israel's Psalmody*, pp. 167ff. There is no support for changing the pointing of רבד and the need to smooth the text is answered by the description of the structure of the psalm contained herein.

69. Cf. Baumann, *ZAW*, 1950, p. 120.

70. Cf. Kraus, *Psalmen*, p. 430, who relates the conclusion of the psalm to the holy war tradition.

71. This is in opposition to the doubt expressed by Johnson, *Cultic Prophet and Israel's Psalmody*, pp. 172ff., who also sees this whole psalm as the comforting work of a cult prophet in time of war.

72. Cf. Gunkel, *Die Psalmen*, p. 475.

73. Cf. Baumann, *ZAW*, 1950, p. 122; Mowinckel, *The Psalms in Israel's Worship* II, p. 59.

74. Eaton, *Kingship and the Psalms*, p. 60, understands the introductory praise to have the character of testimony to Yahweh's past action for the worshipper. Eaton also claims that Ps. 108 is a 'royal' composition. The psalm clearly refers to a military crisis involving the whole community but does that necessarily make it 'royal'?

75. Pss. 60.6; 85.8 might indicate an experience of audition but the language is stylized enough to make that questionable.

Notes to Excursus II

1. Cf. A.A. Anderson, *Psalms* I, p. 28.
2. Cf. *ibid.*; E. Podechard, *Le Psautier* I, 1949, pp. 33f.; James F. Ross, 'Job 33:14-30: The Phenomenology of Lament', *JBL* 94, 1975, pp. 44f.; Weiser, *The Psalms*, pp. 426, 458.
3. Cf. Weiser, *The Psalms*, pp. 73ff. He also notes some possible slight influence from the cults of the dying and rising vegetation gods in the lamenter's assured deliverance from the underworld.
4. 'A Study in the Form Criticism of Individual Complaint Psalms', *VT* 6, 1956, pp. 80-96; cf. Otto Kaiser, *Introduction to the Old Testament*, 1975, p. 335.
5. Cf. *Prayer*, 1932; Gunkel—Begrich, pp. 245ff.; Westermann, *The Praise of God*, pp. 65, 70; also J. Alberto Soggin, *Introduction to the Old Testament*, 1976, p. 373.
6. 'Das Priesterliche Orakel in Israel und Juda', *BZAW* 33, 1918, pp. 285-301. Note especially p. 300 where he cites prophetic texts opposing the priestly oracle as support for his position.
7. Cf. Gunkel—Begrich, pp. 245ff.; Westermann, *The Praise of God*, pp. 65, 70, 73. Could the oracle also perhaps bring about what Westermann calls 'declarative praise', the thanksgiving or praise found in laments which have already been answered? Cf., for example, Pss. 6; 10. Cf. pp. 34, 80, 102, 105f.; Mowinckel, *The Psalms in Israel's Worship* I, pp. 218f., 234f. and II, pp. 11, 59. Also cf. Gerhard von Rad, *Old Testament Theology* I, p. 401; Christoph Barth, *Introduction to the Psalms*, pp. 16f., Hempel, *IDB* III, p. 951; G.R. Driver, 'The Psalms in the Light of Babylonian Research', *The Psalmists*, ed. D.C. Simpson, 1926, p. 159; Aage Bentzen, *Introduction to the Old Testament* I, pp. 158f.; more tentatively Helmer Ringgren, *The Faith of the Psalmists*, p. 76; Otto Eissfeldt, *The Old Testament: An Introduction*, 1965, pp. 117f.; Soggin, *Introduction to the Old Testament*, p. 373.
8. 'Das Priesterliche Heilsorakel', *ZAW* 52, 1934, pp. 81-92; *Studien zu Deuterojesaja*, 1938.
9. Other passages which Begrich treats are Is. 41.14-16; 43.1-3a, 5; (44.2-5); 48.17-19; 49.7, 14-15; 51.7-8; 54.4-8; Jer. 30.10, 11=46.27, 28. Begrich's comments on vocabulary, form and tense are particularly helpful. He also notes simple ways the prophet expands the oracle.
10. Cf. Begrich, *Der Psalm des Hiskia*, 1926. It is intriguing to speculate whether Begrich's work on Is. 38 might have influenced his research on the *Heilsorakel*. Vv. 4ff. are particularly relevant here though the form of the expression of certainty in vv. 17ff. is still clearly psalmic. The reference to the oracle in the narrative of Is. 38 also perhaps moves us closer to the prophetic experience behind such an oracle of, assurance (cf. p. 77 above).
11. Cf. Begrich, *Der Psalm des Hiskia*, pp. 51, 53, 61; Fohrer, *Das Buch Jesaja* II, 1972, p. 188; W. Stärk, *Lyrik*, p. 197; A.S. Herbert, *The Book of the*

Prophet Isaiah, Chapters 1-39, 1973, p. 212; Scott, *IB* V, p. 374; Seybold, *Das Gebet den Kranken*, pp. 147ff.; P.A.H. de Boer, 'Notes on Text and Meaning of Isaiah XXXVIII 9-20', *OTS* 9, 1951, p. 185; Delekat, *Asylie und Schutzorakel*, pp. 4, 21.

12. The view taken here is that the change of mood occurs between the petition in v. 16 and the expression of certainty in v. 17 (cf. pp. 80f. below). Cf. Josef Linder, 'Textkritische und exegetische Studie zum Canticum Ezechiae (Is. 38, 9-20)', *ZKTh* 42, 1918, pp. 60ff.; Samuel Daiches, 'Isaiah XXXVIII.15, 16', *ExpT* 25, 1913-1914, p. 564; John Mauchline, *Isaiah 1-39*, 1962, pp. 235f.; also Otto Kaiser, *Isaiah 13-39*, 1974, p. 406; H.S. Nyberg, 'Hiskias Danklied Jes. 38,9-20', *ASTI* 9, 1974, p. 87. Others suggest that the change to thanksgiving comes in v. 15; cf. Begrich, *Der Psalm des Hiskia*, pp. 41ff.; Fohrer, *Das Buch Jesaja* II, p. 190; Otto Procksch, *Jesaja* I, 1930, p. 465; Franz Delitzsch, *Biblical Commentary on the Prophecies of Isaiah* II, 1892, pp. 48f.; Seybold, *Das Gebet den Kranken*, p. 150.

13. Cf. Seybold, *Das Gebet den Kranken*, p. 153; Linder, *ZKTh*, 1918, pp. 47ff.; Stärk, *Lyrik*, pp. 197f.; Duhm, *Das Buch Jesaja*, 1892, pp. 255f.; Westermann, *The Praise of God*, p. 80, footnote 27. Others, however, understand the psalm as a prayer of thanksgiving; Begrich, *Der Psalm des Hiskia*, pp. 17ff.; Kaiser, *Isaiah 13-39*, p. 404; Mauchline, *Isaiah 1-39*, p. 235; Frank Crüsemann, *Studien zur Formgeschichte von Hymnus und Danklied in Israel*, 1969, pp. 239ff.; Fohrer, *Das Buch Jesaja* II, p. 188.

14. *Das Buch Jesaja* II, p. 188; cf. Begrich, *Der Psalm des Hiskia*, pp. 53f.

15. It may be that an extra מר has come into the text but the two could indicate emphasis; cf. de Boer, *OTS*, 1951, p. 183. It is also possible that מר is a verb from the root מור, indicating the change from bitterness to prosperity.

16. Literally, 'in respect to prosperity'. The ל carries a kind of contrasting force, 'instead of'.

17. Though not in the translation given here, חשקת is often emended to חשבת; cf. *BHS*. Begrich, *Der Psalm des Hiskia*, p. 48, sees the text as impossible though Nyberg, *ASTI*, 1974, p. 95, accepts it as the more difficult reading. The translation is explained below.

18. The negative refers to both parts of the line; *G-K*, par. 152z.

19. Some emend אמתך to חסדך (cf. v. 19; the familiar word pair would then be present); cf. Begrich, *Der Psalm des Hiskia*, p. 49. The Septuagint may support that; cf. *BHS*. However the sense of אמתך is still in line with the Greek; it is what the delivered person remembers in v. 19 and what those in Sheol do not experience.

20. Cf. Westermann, *The Praise of God*, p. 71.

21. Cf. *ibid.*, p. 102; Seybold, *Das Gebet den Kranken*, p. 150.

22. Begrich, *Der Psalm des Hiskia*, pp. 59f., understands the sins involved to be those hidden from the worshipper but not from God. They are probably to be regarded as the cause for his sickness or misfortune.

23. Cf. *BDB*, pp. 365f.; *K-B*, p. 342.

24. Cf. Pss. 31.22f.; 55.17ff. No enemies are mentioned in Is. 38.17f. but this is also the case in some of the expressions of certainty in the Psalter.

25. Delekat, *Asylie und Schutzorakel*; Beyerlin, *Die Rettung der Bedrängten*; Seybold, *Das Gebet den Kranken*; cf. Hans Schmidt, *Die Religiöse Lyrik*, p. 26.

26. Cf. H.M. Dion, 'The Patriarchal Traditions and the Literary Form of the "Oracle of Salvation"', *CBQ* 29, 1967, pp. 198-206, and Gen. 26.23-25; Deut. 3.2; Josh. 8.1-2; Judges 6.23; Jer. 1.6-8; II Kings 19.1-7; also Ps. 118.5-6.

27. Cf. Morris Jastrow, Jr., *The Religion of Babylonia and Assyria*, 1898, pp. 343-344; Philip B. Harner, 'The Salvation Oracle in Second Isaiah', *JBL* 88, 1969, pp. 418ff.; James B. Pritchard (ed.), *ANET*, 1955, pp. 449-451; note the use of 'fear not', the emphasis on protection and false accusation (p. 450); also cf. I Sam. 1 with p. 450; H.-J. Zobel, 'Das Gebet um Abwendung der Not und seine Erhörung in den Klageliedern des Alten Testaments und in der Inschrift des Königs Zakir von Hamath', *VT* 21, 1971, pp. 91-99.

28. Weiser, *The Psalms*, pp. 79f.; Rudolf Kilian, 'Ps 22 und das priesterliche Heilsorakel', *BZ*, n.f. 12, 1968, pp. 172-185; cf. S.B. Frost, 'Asseveration by Thanksgiving', *VT* 8, 1958, pp. 380-390. Frost's position still does not really explain what brought about the certainty.

29. Cf. Gunkel—Begrich, p. 247, where he says the cultic style of the lament remained in use even after the psalms were freed from the cult; cf. Weiser, *The Psalms*, pp. 79f.; Ridderbos, *Die Psalmen*, 1972, p. 71, who often accounts for the certainty of a hearing with a redaction of the texts to bring them in line with the cultic ritual.

30. Cf. Zobel, *VT*, 1971, pp. 97ff.; this, of course, is also the view of Küchler, Gunkel, Begrich and others. The use of oracles was part of the priestly function.

Notes to Chapter Four

1. *Psalmenstudien* III, pp. 27ff.

2. Emil Balla, 'Habakuk', *RGG* II, second edition, 1928, cols. 1556f. Paul Humbert, *Problèmes du Livre d'Habacuc*, 1944, especially pp. 247, 284f., 289.

3. Cf., for example, Sigmund Mowinckel, 'Zum Psalm des Habakuk', *ThZ* 9, 1953, pp. 3f., 8, 23; Karl Elliger, *Das Buch der zwölf Kleinen Propheten* II, 1956, pp. 24ff., 55; Otto Kaiser, *Introduction to the Old Testament*, pp. 236f.; J.H. Eaton, 'The Origin and Meaning of Habakkuk 3', *ZAW* 76, 1964, pp. 144ff. and *Festal Drama in Deutero-Isaiah*, pp. 36, 110f.; Aage Bentzen, *Introduction to the Old Testament* II, 1967, p. 152. Contrast Carl-A. Keller, 'Die Eigenart der Prophetie Habakuks', *ZAW* 85, 1973,

pp. 163ff.; Wilhelm Rudolph, *Micha-Nahum-Habakuk-Zephanja*, 1975, p. 194. Cf. Ed. Nielsen, 'The Righteous and the Wicked in Habaqquq', *StTh* 6, 1952, pp. 54ff.

4. The use of the perfect here apparently indicates that the prophet has been calling upon Yahweh for some time.

5. The entire verse is understood as a question. שׂא is awkward here because there is no object and the reading *BHS* suggests is attractive. However we have kept the text as indicating that strife has lifted up itself in boldness and independence, unusual in the *qal* but similar to the verb's use with terms such as head, heart; cf. *BDB*, pp. 670f.

6. Cf. Rudolph, *Micha-Nahum-Habakuk-Zephanja*, pp. 200f.; John D.W. Watts, *The Books of Joel, Obadiah, Jonah, Nahum, Habakkuk and Zephaniah*, 1975, p. 125.

7. Cf. Pss. 10.1; 12.6; 27.12; 28.1f.; 140.

8. V. 16 speaks of the profound effect of the vision on the person of the prophet and moves quickly to the expression of certainty.

9. The enemy in chapter 3 is the same as in chapter 2, and it may be that the vision of chapter 3 is related to the one mentioned in chapter 2 but this is less than certain. We are treating the psalm of Habakkuk in a holistic fashion, concentrating on the form of the text in Habakkuk 3.

10. Cf. Pss. 12.6f.; 27.6; 28.6f.; 31.22f.; 55.19.

11. Cf. Rudolph, *Micha-Nahum-Habakuk-Zephanja*, pp. 201f., 205. Hans Schmidt's view in 'Ein Psalm im Buche Habakuk', *ZAW* 62, 1950, pp. 52ff., would tend to support this though the results of Schmidt's investigation are extremely dubious.

12. There are mythical and cultic elements in the psalm of chapter 3 but the prophet uses these for the purpose noted here. Contrast W. Staerk, 'Zu Habakuk 1:5-11. Geschichte oder Mythos?' *ZAW* 51, 1933, pp. 1ff.

13. William A. Irwin, 'The Psalm of Habakkuk', *JNES* I, 1942, p. 39. This concluding certainty of a hearing is, as we have seen, in response to the prophet's vision in which he was shown the victory. It could be said that the vision performs the function of a *Heilsorakel*.

14. Mowinckel, *ThZ*, 1953, pp. 21f.; Rudolph, *Micha-Nahum-Habakuk-Zephanja*, p. 248; cf. Schmidt, *ZAW*, 1950, p. 62.

15. Jeremias, *Kultprophetie und Gerichtsverkündigung*, pp. 5ff.; cf. especially pp. 76ff., concludes that Habakkuk is a cult prophet. Rudolph *Micha-Nahum-Habakkuk-Zephanja*, p. 194, takes the opposite view. With Rudolph, a date around 600 B.C. seems best for Habakkuk's prophecy.

16. Even Rudolph indicates that the psalm in Hab. 3 was used in worship, *Micha-Nahum-Habakkuk-Zephanja*, pp. 240, 250. It also probably needs to be said that attempts to deal with the relationship of psalmody and prophecy, in this case having to do with Habakkuk, in terms of the categories of prophets of weal and prophets of woe are simply inadequate. Such categories are not really appropriate for the prophetic material.

17. Even Eaton notes the prophetic character of the book, *ZAW*, 1964, pp. 166ff.

18. This is sometimes said to relate Habakkuk to Israel's wisdom traditions; cf. Keller, *ZAW*, 1973, pp. 162f.

19. We have noted the use of the rhetorical question in the lament psalms but the point here is its frequency in Habakkuk. It predominates more than in the Psalms.

20. Cf. Georg Fohrer, 'Remarks on Modern Interpretation of the Prophets', *JBL* 80, 1961, pp. 309ff.

21. Cf. also Moshe Weinfeld, 'Ancient Near Eastern Patterns in Prophetic Literature', *VT* 27, 1977, pp. 189, 195; Erhard Gerstenberger, 'The Woe-Oracles of the Prophets', *JBL* 81, 1962, pp. 253-255, 263; James Muilenburg, 'The 'Office' of the Prophet in Ancient Israel', *The Bible in Modern Scholarship*, ed. James Philip Hyatt, 1965, p. 89; Keller, *ZAW*, 1973, pp. 165ff.; Elliger, *Kleinen Propheten* II, p. 26; Baruch Margulis, 'The Psalm of Habakkuk: A Reconstruction and Interpretation', *ZAW* 82, 1970, p. 411; Ferris J. Stephens, 'The Babylonian Dragon Myth in Habakkuk 3', *JBL* 43, 1924, pp. 292f., takes the view that even extra-biblical sources were used in Hab. 3; further, William Hayes Ward, *A Critical and Exegetical Commentary on Habakkuk*, 1912, p. 7, takes the view that much of the book was 'compiled and edited' by Habakkuk.

22. Similar conclusions are appropriate in reference to Nahum's use of psalmic material, especially the hymnic material in chapter 1.

23. *Psalmenstudien* III, p. 29. This assessment of Joel has its background in the work of Baumgartner, 'Joel 1 und 2', *Karl Budde zum siebzigsten Geburtstag*, ed. Karl Marti, 1920, pp. 10ff., who relates Joel to the Psalms and lament liturgy; cf. Gunkel, *The Psalms*, p. 13; Ivan Engnell, *Studies in Divine Kingship in the Ancient Near East*, 1967, p. 159.

24. *Joel Studies*, 1948, pp. 4, 6, 11. Cf. G.W. Ahlström, *Joel and the Temple Cult of Jerusalem*, 1971, p. 32; Rudolph, *Joel-Amos-Obadja-Jona*, 1971, pp. 26f. It is interesting to note how Rudolph's attitude concerning Joel differs from his work on other prophetic books. Cf. also Ernst Kutsch, 'Heuschrecken-plage und Tag Jahwes in Joel 1 and 2', *ThZ* 18, 1962, pp. 81f.

25. H.W. Wolff has expressed some doubts about this view; cf. *Joel and Amos*, 1977, pp. 11, 24f.

26. Cf. Kapelrud, *Joel Studies*, pp. 50, 192f.; Miloš Bič, *Das Buch Joel*, 1960, especially pp. 106ff.; Ahlström, *Joel and the Temple Cult*, pp. 21f.; Rudolph, *Joel-Amos-Obadja-Jona*, pp. 26f.

27. Wolff, *Joel and Amos*, pp. 4-6; cf. Soggin, *Introduction to the Old Testament*, pp. 352ff. For two differing post-exilic datings, cf. Marco Treves, 'The Date of Joel', *VT* 7, 1957, pp. 149ff.; Jacob M. Myers, 'Some Considerations Bearing on the Date of Joel', *ZAW* 74, 1962, pp. 177ff., who also comments on Joel's relationship to the cult.

28. Cf. Soggin, *Introduction to the Old Testament*, pp. 353f.; Wolff, *Joel and Amos*, p. 5; Ahlström, *Joel and the Temple Cult*, pp. 11ff.

29. Also pertinent is the presence of some material in Joel which tends toward apocalyptic.

30. Cf. Wolff, *Joel and Amos*, p. 22; Ahlström, *Joel and the Temple Cult*, pp. 130f.

31. Wolff, *Joel and Amos*, p. 22.

32. Cf. *ibid.*, p. 23; Pss. 85; 126.

33. Though it is described in a different way, the figurative language here still pertains to the agricultural crisis at hand; cf. Joel 2.3, 5, 19ff.

34. For a different view, cf. Karl Budde, 'Der Umschwung in Joel 2', *OLZ* 22, 1919, cols. 104ff.

35. C . Wolff, *Joel and Amos*, p. 57, and Bič, *Joel*, pp. 65f.

36. Cf. Pss. 12; 60; 85; 108; Baumgartner, *Karl Budde zum siebzigstem Geburtstag*, pp. 14, 16; Kapelrud, *Joel Studies*, pp. 4, 6, 90, 92; Wolff, *Joel and Amos*, p. 58.

37. Cf. Wolff, *Joel and Amos*, p. 59; Rudolph, *Joel-Amos-Obadja-Jona*, pp. 65f.

38. The 'Northerner' here has a mythic and apocalyptic background and thus implications beyond the locusts but they are the current manifestation of that opposition; cf. Wolff, *Joel and Amos*, p. 62. This is in opposition to Rudolph, *Joel-Amos-Obadja-Jona*, p. 63; Budde, "Der von Norden' in Joel 2,20', *OLZ* 22, 1919, cols. 1ff.; Bič, *Joel*, pp. 69ff., who again relates this to a context of battle with fertility religion.

39. Cf. Rudolph, *Joel-Amos-Obadja-Jona*, pp. 24, 66, 68; Bič, *Joel*, pp. 73f., who sees this in terms of Yahweh's granting fertility rather than Baal's.

40. Cf. Bič, *Joel*, p. 81, who again contrasts this with Baal's endowing of ecstasy.

41. Cf. Rudolph, *Joel-Amos-Obadja-Jona*, p. 63. We are thus still dealing with the uniform phenomenon of certainty which we have been considering throughout our investigation.

42. Cf. Wolff *Joel and Amos*, p. 68.

43. Wolff, *Joel and Amos*, p. 9; also especially cf. p. 10.

44. There are a number of additional texts in Isaiah which illustrate this conclusion, often in relation to psalms of thanksgiving—Is. 12 and several texts in Is. 24–27.

Notes to Chapter Five

1. It is exceedingly difficult to specify the nature of this renewal/protection, in part because of the figurative language involved.

2. Cf. B.D. Napier, 'Prophet, Prophetism', *IDB* III, p. 902, and his statement: 'To entertain reservations as to the great prophets' membership

in the guilds of the professional cult prophets is in no sense at all, then, to cut the prophet off from influential and productive interrelationship in the cult'.

3. One possible area for productive research on these questions is the book of Lamentations since it apparently relates to a ritual enacted on the site of the ruins of the temple and to the historical occurrence of the fall of Jerusalem. It includes psalmic and prophetic elements akin to those we have been investigating.

Abbreviations

AJSL	*American Journal of Semitic Language and Literatures*, Chicago
ANET	Pritchard. *Ancient Near Eastern Texts*
ASTI	*Annual of the Swedish Theological Institute*, Leiden
BA	*Biblical Archaeologist*, Cambridge, Massachusetts
BASOR	*Bulletin of the American Schools of Oriental Research*, Baltimore
BDB	Brown, Driver and Briggs. *Hebrew and English Lexicon*
BHS	*Biblia Hebraica Stuttgartensia*, 1967-77
BJRL	*Bulletin of the John Rylands University Library of Manchester*
BKAT	*Biblischer Kommentar Altes Testament*
BR	*Biblical Research*, Chicago
BWANT	Beiträge zur Wissenschaft vom Alten und Neuen Testament
BZ	*Biblische Zeitschrift*, Paderborn
BZAW	Beiheft zur *Zeitschrift für die alttestamentliche Wissenschaft*
CBC	Cambridge Bible Commentary
CBQ	*Catholic Biblical Quarterly*, Washington
EThL	*Ephemerides Theologicae Lovanienses*, Louvain
ExpT	*Expository Times*, Edinburgh
FRLANT	Forschungen zur Religion und Literatur des Alten und Neuen Testaments
G-K	Gesenius—Kautzsch. *Hebrew Grammar*
HTR	*Harvard Theological Review*, Cambridge, Massachusetts
HUCA	*Hebrew Union College Annual*, Cincinnati
IB	*Interpreter's Bible*
IDB	*Interpreter's Dictionary of the Bible*, New York and Nashville
JBL	*Journal of Biblical Literature*, Missoula, Montana
JNES	*Journal of Near Eastern Studies*, Chicago
JQR	*Jewish Quarterly Review*, Philadelphia
JR	*Journal of Religion*, Chicago
JTS	*Journal of Theological Studies*, Oxford

K-B	Köhler—Baumgartner, *Lexicon in Veteris Testamenti Libros*
MT	Masoretic Text
NEB	*New English Bible*, 1970
OLZ	*Orientalistische Literaturzeitung*, Leipzig
OTL	Old Testament Library
OTS	*Oudtestamentische Studiën*, Leiden
RB	*Revue Biblique*, Paris
RGG	*Religion in Geschichte und Gegenwart*, Tübingen
RSV	*Revised Standard Version*, 1952 (1959 edition)
SBT	Studies in Biblical Theology
SJT	*Scottish Journal of Theology*, Edinburgh
SMB	*Studien und Mitteilungen aus dem Benediktiner- und dem Cistercienser-Orden*, Brünn
StTh	*Studia Theologica*, Lund
SVT	Supplements to *Vetus Testamentum*
TDNT	*Theological Dictionary of the New Testament*, Grand Rapids, Michigan
TDOT	*Theological Dictionary of the Old Testament*, Grand Rapids, Michigan
TGUOS	*Transactions of the Glasgow University Oriental Society*, Leiden
THAT	*Theologisches Handwörterbuch zum Alten Testament*, München
ThLZ	*Theologische Literaturzeitung*, Berlin
ThQ	*Theologische Quartalschrift*, Stuttgart
ThZ	*Theologische Zeitschrift*, Basel
TWAT	*Theologisches Wörterbuch zum Alten Testament*
TWNT	*Theologisches Wörterbuch zum Neuen Testament*
VT	*Vetus Testamentum*, Leiden
WMANT	Wissenschaftliche Monographien zum Alten und Neuen Testament
ZAW	*Zeitschrift für die alttestamentliche Wissenschaft*, Berlin
ZKTh	*Zeitschrift für katholische Theologie*, Innsbruck
ZST	*Zeitschrift für systematische Theologie*, Berlin
ZThK	*Zeitschrift für Theologie und Kirche*, Tübingen

BIBLIOGRAPHY

Psalm Commentaries

Anderson, A.A. *The Book of Psalms* (New Century Bible). London: Oliphants, 1972, 2 vols.

Anderson, G.W. 'The Psalms', *Peake's Commentary on the Bible*. London: Thomas Nelson and Sons Ltd., 1962.

Baethgen, Frdr. *Die Psalmen* (Handkommentar zum Alten Testament II, 2). Göttingen: Vandenhoeck & Ruprecht, 1892.

Barnes, W.E. *The Psalms* (Westminster Commentaries). London: Methuen & Co. Ltd., 1931.

Betholet, A. 'Das Buch der Psalmen', *Die Heilige Schrift des Alten Testaments* II, 4th ed. Tübingen: J.C.B. Mohr (Paul Siebeck), 1923.

Boylan, Patrick *The Psalms: A Study of the Vulgate in the Light of the Hebrew Text*. Dublin: M.H. Gill and Sons Ltd., 1920-1924, 2 vols.

Briggs, C.A. and E.G. *A Critical and Exegetical Commentary on the Book of Psalms* (The International Critical Commentary). Edinburgh: T. & T. Clark, 1906-1907, 2 vols.

Buttenwieser, Moses *The Psalms Chronologically Treated with a New Translation*. Chicago: The University of Chicago, 1938.

Cheyne, T.K. *The Book of Psalms*. London: Kegan, Paul, Trench, Trübner & Co. Ltd., 1904.

Cohen, A., (ed.) *The Psalms*. Hindhead, Surrey: The Soncino Press, 1945.

Dahood, Mitchell *Psalms* (The Anchor Bible). Garden City, New York: Doubleday & Co., 1966-1970, 3 vols.

Davison, W.T., (ed.) *The Psalms* (The Century Bible). London: Caxton Publishing Company, n.d., vol. 1.

Deissler, Alfons *Die Psalmen* (Die Welt der Bibel). Düsseldorf: Patmos-Verlag, 1963-1965, 3 vols.

Delitzsch, Franz *Biblical Commentary on the Psalms*. Trans., David Eaton. London: Hodder and Stoughton, 1902. [*Commentar ueber den Psalter*. Leipzig: Doerffling und Franke, 1859.]

Drijvers, Pius *The Psalms: Their Structure and Meaning*. London: Burns and Oates, 1965.

Duhm, Bernh. *Die Psalmen* (Kurzer Hand-Commentar zum Alten Testament 14). 2nd ed. Tübingen: J.C.B. Mohr (Paul Siebeck), 1922.

Durham, John I. 'Psalms', *The Broadman Bible Commentary*, IV. London: Marshall, Morgan & Scott, 1971.

Eaton, J.H. *Psalms* (Torch Bible Commentaries). London: SCM Press Ltd., 1967.

Eerdmans, B.D. *The Hebrew Book of Psalms* (OTS 4). Leiden: E.J. Brill, 1947.

Gunkel, Hermann *Die Psalmen* (Göttinger Handkommentar zum Alten Testament II, 2, 4th ed.). Göttingen: Vandenhoeck & Ruprecht, 1926.

Kirkpatrick, A.F., (ed.) *The Book of Psalms* (The Cambridge Bible for Schools and Colleges). Cambridge: The University Press, 1902.

Kissane, Edward J. *The Book of Psalms*. Dublin: Browne and Nolan Limited, 1953-1954, 2 vols.

Kittel, Rudolf *Die Psalmen* (Kommentar zum Alten Testament 13, 4th ed.). Leipzig: A. Deichertsche Verlagsbuchhandlung, 1922.

Kraus, Hans-Joachim *Psalmen* (Biblischer Kommentar Altes Testament). Neukirchen Kreis Moers: Neukirchener Verlag, 1960, 2 vols.

Leslie, Elmer A. *The Psalms Translated and Interpreted in the Light of Hebrew Life and Worship*. New York: Abingdon-Cokesbury Press, 1949.

Murphy, Roland E. 'Psalms', *The Jerome Biblical Commentary*. London: Geoffrey Chapman, 1968.

Oesterley, W.O.E. *The Psalms*. London: SPCK, 1953.

Podechard, E. *Le Psautier I: traduction littérale et explication historique*. Lyon: Facultés Catholiques, 1949.

Rogerson, J.W. and McKay, J.W. *Psalms* (CBC). Cambridge: The University Press, 1977, 3 vols.

Sabourin, Leopold *The Psalms: Their Origin and Meaning*. Staten Island, New York: Alba House, 1969.

Schmidt, Hans *Die Psalmen* (Handbuch zum Alten Testament I, 15). Tübingen: J.C.B. Mohr (Paul Siebeck), 1934.

Stärk, W. *Lyrik: Psalmen, Hoheslied und Verwandtes* (Die Schriften des Alten Testaments III, 1). Göttingen: Vandenhoeck & Ruprecht, 1911.

Taylor, William R. and McCullough, W. Stewart 'The Book of Psalms' (Exegesis), *IB* IV. New York and Nashville: Abingdon Press, 1955.

Weiser, Artur. *The Psalms: A Commentary* (OTL). London: SCM Press Ltd., 1959. [*Die Psalmen* (Das Alte Testament Deutsch 14/15) 5th ed. Göttingen: Vandenhoeck & Ruprecht, 1959.]

Wutz, Franz. *Die Psalmen*. München: Kösel & Pustet, 1925.

Other Sources

Abbott, T.K. 'On the Alphabetical Arrangement of Psalms IX and X with Some Other Emendations', *ZAW* 16 (1896), 292-294.

Ackroyd, P.R. 'An Interpretation of the Babylonian Exile: A Study of 2 Kings 20, Isaiah 38, 39', *SJT* 27 (1974), 329-352.

Ahlström, G.W. *Joel and the Temple Cult of Jerusalem* (SVT 21). Leiden: E.J. Brill, 1971.

Albright, W.F. 'The Psalm of Habakkuk', *Studies in Old Testament Prophecy Presented to Theodore H. Robinson*. Ed., H.H. Rowley. Edinburgh: T. & T. Clark, 1950: 1-18.

Anderson, George W. 'Enemies and Evildoers in the Book of Psalms', *BJRL* 48 (1965-1966), 18-29.

Balla, Emil 'Habakuk', *RGG* II, 2nd ed. (1928), cols. 1556-1557.

—*Das Ich der Psalmen* (FRLANT 16). Göttingen: Vandenhoeck & Ruprecht, 1912.

Barr, James *The Semantics of Biblical Language*. London: Oxford University Press, 1962.

Barth, Christoph *Die Errettung vom Tode in den Individuellen Klage-und Dankliedern des Altes Testaments*. Zollikon: Evangelischer Verlag A.G., 1947.

—*Introduction to the Psalms*. Trans., R.A. Wilson. Oxford: Basil Blackwell, 1966. [*Einfuehrung in die Psalmen*, Neukirchen-Vluyn: Neukirchener Verlag, 1961.]

Baumann, Eberhard 'שוב שבות Eine exegetische Untersuchung', *ZAW* 47 (1929), 17-44.

—'Struktur-Untersuchungen im Psalter I', *ZAW* 61 (1945/48), 114-176.

—'Struktur-Untersuchungen im Psalter II', *ZAW* 62 (1950), 115-152.

Baumgartner, Walter 'Joel 1 und 2', *Karl Budde zum siebsigsten Geburtstag* (BZAW 34). Ed. Karl Marti. Giessen: Alfred Topelmann, 1920, 10-19.

Becker, Joachim *Israel Deutet seine Psalmen: Urform und Neuinterpretation in den Psalmen* (Stuttgarter Bibelstudien 18). Stuttgart: Katholisches Bibelwerk, 1966.

—*Wege der Psalmenexegese* (Stuttgarter Bibelstudien 78). Stuttgart: KBW Verlag, 1975.

Begrich, Joachim 'Das Priesterliche Heilsorakel', *ZAW* 52 (1934), 81-92.

—*Der Psalm des Hiskia: Ein Beitrag zum Verständnis von Jesaja 38, 10-20* (FRLANT 42). Göttingen: Vandenhoeck & Ruprecht, 1926.

—*Studien zu Deuterojesaja* (BWANT IV, 25). Stuttgart: W. Kohlhammer, 1938.

—'Die Vertrauensäusserungen im israelitischen Klageliede des Einzelnen und in seinen babylonischen Gegenstück', *ZAW* 46 (1928), 221-260.

Bennett, Robert A. 'Wisdom Motifs in Psalm 14-53—*nābāl* and *'ēṣāh*', *BASOR* 220 (1975), 15-21.

Bentzen, Aage *Introduction to the Old Testament*. 7th ed. Copenhagen: G.E.C. Gad Publisher, 1967, 2 vols.

—*King and Messiah* (Lutterworth Studies in Church and Bible). London: Lutterworth Press, 1955. [*Messias-Moses Redivivus-Menchensohn*, Zürich: Zwingli, 1948.]

Bewer, Julius A. *A Critical and Exegetical Commentary on Obadiah and Joel* (International Critical Commentary). Edinburgh: T. & T. Clark, 1912.

Beyerlin, Walter *Die Rettung der Bedrängten in den Feindpsalmen der Einzelnen auf institutionelle Zusammenhänge untersucht* (FRLANT 99). Göttingen: Vandenhoeck & Ruprecht, 1970.

—'Die *tôdā* der Heilsvergegenwärtigung in den Klageliedern des Einzelnen', *ZAW* 79 (1967), 208-224.

—*We are like Dreamers*. Edinburgh: T. & T. Clark, 1982.

Bič, Miloš. *Das Buch Joel*. Berlin: Evangelische Verlagsanstalt, 1960.

Birkeland, Harris *The Evildoers in the Book of Psalms* (Avhandlinger utgitt av Det Norske Videnskaps-Akademi i Oslo II. Hist.-Filos. Klasse, No. 2). Oslo: Jacob Dybwad, 1955.

de Boer, P.A.H. 'Notes on the Text and Meaning of Isaiah XXXVIII 9-20', *OTS* 9 (1951), 170-186.

Box, G.H. *The Book of Isaiah*. London: Sir Isaac Pitman and Sons Ltd., 1908.

Brockelmann, Carl *Hebräische Syntax*. Neukirchen Kreis Moers: Verlag der Buchhandlung des Erziehungsvereins, 1956.

Brown, Francis; Driver, S.R.; and Briggs, Charles A. *A Hebrew and English Lexicon of the Old Testament*. Oxford: The Clarendon Press, 1907.

Brownlee, William H. 'The Placarded Revelation of Habakkuk', *JBL* 82 (1962), 319-325.

Brueggemann, Walter 'From Hurt to Joy, From Death to Life', *Interpretation* 28 (1974), 3-19.

Buber, Martin *Right and Wrong: An Interpretation of Some Psalms*. Trans., Ronald Gregor Smith. London: SCM Press Ltd., 1952.

Budde, Karl 'Psalm 14 und 53', *JBL* 47 (1928), 160-183.

—'Psalm Problems. II. Psalms XIV and LIII', *ExpT* 12 (1900/01), 285-288.

—'Der von Norden in Joel 2,20', *OLZ* 22 (1919), cols. 1-5.

—'Der Umschwung in Joel 2', *OLZ* 22 (1919), cols. 104-110.

Cannon, W.W. 'The Integrity of Habakkuk cc. 1.2', *ZAW* 43 (1925), 62-90.

Cassirer, Ernst *Language and Myth*. Trans., Suzanne K. Langer. New York: Dover Publications Inc., 1946. [*Sprache und Mythos* (Studien der Bibliothek Warburgh 6) Leipzig: B.G. Teubner, 1925.]

Cheyne, T.K. *The Prophecies of Isaiah* I. 3rd ed. London: Kegan, Paul, Trench & Co., 1884.

Childs, Brevard S. *Exodus: A Commentary* (OTL). London: SCM Press Ltd., 1974.

—*Isaiah and the Assyrian Crisis* (SBT, second series, 3). London: SCM Press Ltd., 1967.

Clements, Ronald E. *A Century of Old Testament Study*. London: Lutterworth Press, 1976.

—*Prophecy and Covenant* (SBT, first series, 43). London: SCM Press Ltd., 1965.

—'Temple and Land: A Significant Aspect of Israel's Worship', *TGUOS* XIX (1963), 16-28.

Crüsemann, Frank *Studien zur Formgeschichte von Hymnus und Danklied in Israel* (WMANT 32). Neukirchen-Vluyn: Neukirchener Verlag, 1969.

Culley, Robert C. *Oral Formulaic Language in the Biblical Psalms*. Toronto: University of Toronto Press, 1967.

Dahood, Mitchell חדל' "Cessation" in Isaiah 38,11', *Biblica* 52 (1971), 215-216.

Daiches, Samuel 'Isaiah XXXVIII.15,16', *ExpT* 25 (1913/14), 564.

Davidson, A.B. *Hebrew Syntax*. 3rd ed. Edinburgh: T. & T. Clark, 1902.

—*An Introductory Hebrew Grammar*. 24th ed. rev. John McFadyen. Edinburgh: T. & T. Clark, 1947.

Davies, G. Henton *Exodus* (Torch Bible Commentaries). London: SCM Press Ltd., 1967.

Delekat, Lienhard *Asylie und Schutzorakel am Zionheiligtum*. Leiden: E.J. Brill, 1967.

Delitzsch, Franz *Biblical Commentary on the Prophecies of Isaiah* (The Foreign Biblical Library). Trans. James Denney. London: Hodder and Stoughton, 1891-92, 2 vols. [*Biblischer commentar ueber den Prophet Jesaia*, 3rd ed. Leipzig: Doerffling und Franke, 1875.]

Dietrich, Ernst Ludwig שבות שוב *Die Endzeitliche Wiederherstellung bei den Propheten* (BZAW 40). Giessen: Alfred Töpelmann, 1925.

Dillmann, August and Kittel, Rudolf *Der Prophet Jesaja* (Kurzgefasstes exegetisches Handbuch zum Alten Testament 5, 6th ed.). Leipzig: S. Hirzel, 1898.

Dion, Hyacinthe M. 'The Patriarchal Traditions and the Literary Form of the Oracle of Salvation', *CBQ* 29 (1967), 198-206.

Driver, G.R. 'Linguistic and Textual Problems: Isaiah I-XXXIX', *JTS* 38 (1937), 36-50.

—'Notes on the Psalms I. 1-72', *JTS* 43 (1942), 149-160.

—*Problems of the Hebrew Verbal System* (Old Testament Studies 2). Edinburgh: T. & T. Clark, 1938.

—'The Psalms in the Light of Babylonian Research', *The Psalmists*. Ed., D.C. Simpson. London: Oxford University Press (1926), 109-175.

—'Studies in the Vocabulary of the Old Testament. II', *JTS* 32 (1931), 250-257.

—'Studies in the Vocabulary of the Old Testament. IV', *JTS* 33 (1932), 38-47.

Driver, G.R. and Miles, John C. *The Assyrian Laws* (Ancient Codes and Laws of the Near East). Oxford: The Clarendon Press, 1935.

—*The Babylonian Laws* I (Ancient Codes and Laws of the Near East). Oxford: The Clarendon Press, 1952.

Driver, S.R. *A Treatise on the Use of the Tenses in Hebrew and Some Other Syntactical Questions* (Clarendon Press Series). 3rd ed. Oxford: The Clarendon Press, 1892.

Duhm, Bernh. *Das Buch Jesaia* (Handkommentar zum Alten Testament III, 1). Göttingen: Vandenhoeck & Ruprecht, 1892.

Eaton, J.H. *Festal Drama in Deutero-Isaiah*. London: SPCK, 1979.

—'The King as God's Witness', *ASTI* 7 (1970), 25-40.

—*Kingship and the Psalms* (SBT, second series, 32). London: SCM Press Ltd., 1976.

—*Obadiah, Nahum, Habakkuk and Zephaniah* (Torch Bible Commentaries). London: SCM Press Ltd., 1961.

—'The Origin and Meaning of Habakkuk 3', *ZAW* 76 (1964), 144-171.

Eichrodt, Walther *Ezekiel: A Commentary* (OTL). London: SCM Press Ltd., 1970. [*Der Prophet Hesekiel*, Göttingen: 1965-1966.]

—*Theology of the Old Testament* I (OTL). Trans. J.A. Baker. London: SCM Press Ltd., 1961. [*Theologie des Alten Testaments* I, 6th ed. Stuttgart: 1959.]

Eissfeldt, Otto *The Old Testament: An Introduction*. Trans. Peter R. Ackroyd. Oxford: Basil Blackwell, 1965. [*Einleitung in das Alte Testament*, 3rd ed. Tübingen: Mohr, 1964.]

Elliger, Karl *Das Buch der zwölf Kleinen Propheten* II (Das Alte Testament D·utsch 25, 3rd ed.). Göttingen: Vandenhoeck & Ruprecht, 1956.

Emerton, J.A. 'The Textual and Linguistic Problems of Hab. II.4-5', *JTS* n.s. 28 (1977), 1-18.

Engnell, Ivan *Studies in Divine Kingship in the Ancient Near East*. 2nd ed. Oxford: Basil Blackwell, 1967 (1st ed. Uppsala: Almqvist and Wiksells boktr., 1943).

Falk, Ze'ev W. *Hebrew Law in Biblical Times: An Introduction*. Jerusalem: Wahrmann Books, 1964.

Falkenstein, A. and von Soden, W. *Sumerische und Akkadische Hymnen und Gebete* (Die Bibliothek der alten Welt, Reihe der alte Orient). Zürich/Stuttgart: Artemis-Verlag, 1953.

Feldmann, Franz *Das Buch Isaias* (Exegetisches Handbuch zum Alten Testament 14). Münster in Westf.: Der Aschendorffschen Verlagsbuchhandlung, 1925.

Fohrer, Georg *Das Buch Jesaja* I-II (Zürcher Bibelkommentare). Zürich/Stuttgart: Zwingli Verlag, 1960-1962.

—*Introduction to the Old Testament* (initiated by Ernst Sellin). Trans. David E. Green. New York: Abingdon Press, 1968. [*Einleitung in das Alte Testament*, Heidelberg: 1965.]

—'Die Propheten des Alten Testaments im Blickfeld neuer Forschung', *Studien zur alttestamentlichen Prophetie (1949-1965)* (BZAW 99). Berlin: Verlag Alfred Töpelmann, 1967: 1-17.

—'Remarks on Modern Interpretation of the Prophets', *JBL* 80 (1961), 309-319.

Frost, S.B. 'Asseveration by Thanksgiving', *VT* 8 (1958), 380-390.

Gerstenberger, Erhard 'The Woe Oracles of the Prophets', *JBL* 81 (1962), 249-263.

Gesenius' Hebrew Grammar Ed. and enlarged E. Kautzsch. Rev. A.E. Cowley. 2nd ed. Oxford: The Clarendon Press, 1910 (1952 reprint).

Good, E.M. 'Love in the Old Testament', *IDB* III (1962), 164-168.

Gordis, Robert 'Psalm 9-10—A Textual and Exegetical Study', *JQR* 48 (1957-58), 104-122.

Gordon, Cyrus H. 'Biblical Customs and the Nuzu Tablets', *BA* 3 (1940), 1-12.

Gray, George Buchanan *Sacrifice in the Old Testament: Its Theory and Practice*. Oxford: The Clarendon Press, 1925.

Gray, John, ed. *Joshua, Judges and Ruth* (New Century Bible). London: Nelson, 1967 (revised ed. 1977).

—*I & II Kings: A Commentary* (OTL). London: SCM Press Ltd., 1964 (2nd ed. 1971).

Greenberg, Moshe 'The Biblical Conception of Asylum', *JBL* 78 (1959), 125-132.

Gross, H. 'Gab es in Israel ein "prophetisches Amt"?' *EThL* 41 (1965), 5-19.

Gruenthaner, M.J. 'Chaldeans or Macedonians? A Recent Theory on the Prophecy of Habakkuk', *Biblica* 8 (1927), 129-160.

Guillaume, Alfred *Prophecy and Divination Among the Hebrews and Other Semites* (The Bampton Lectures). London: Hodder and Stoughton Ltd., 1938.

Gunkel, Hermann *Ausgewählte Psalmen*. 2nd ed. Göttingen: Vandenhoeck & Ruprecht, 1905.

—'The Poetry of the Psalms: Its Literary History and its Application to the Dating of the Psalms', *Old Testament Essays*. London: Charles Griffin and Company, Ltd, 1927, 118-142.

—*The Psalms: A Form-Critical Introduction* (Facet Books). Trans. Thomas W. Horner. Philadelphia: Fortress Press, 1967. ['Psalmen', *RGG* IV, 2nd ed. (1930), 1609-1630.]

—'The Religion of the Psalms', *What Remains of the Old Testament and Other Essays*. Trans. A.K. Dallas. London: George Allen & Unwin Ltd., 1928, 69-114. ['Die Frömmigkeit der Psalmen', *Die Christliche Welt* 36, 1922.]

Gunkel, Hermann and Begrich, Joachim *Einleitung in die Psalmen*. Göttingen: Vandenhoeck & Ruprecht, 1933 (2nd ed., 1966).

Gunneweg, Antonius H.J. *Mündliche und Schriftliche Tradition der vorexilischen Prophetenbücher als Problem der neueren Prophetenforschung* (FRLANT 73). Göttingen: Vandenhoeck & Ruprecht, 1959.

Haldar, Alfred *Associations of Cult Prophets Among the Ancient Semites*. Uppsala: Almqvist & Wiksells Boktryckeri AB, 1945.

Haran, Menahem 'From Early to Classical Prophecy: Continuity and Change', *VT* 27 (1977), 385-397.

Harner, Philip B. 'The Salvation Oracle in Second Isaiah', *JBL* 88 (1969), 418-434.

Heiler, Friedrich *Prayer: A Study in the History and Psychology of Religion.* Trans. and ed. Samuel McComb, with the assistance of J. Edgar Park. London: Oxford University Press, 1932.

Hempel, Johannes *Die althebräische Literatur und ihr hellenistisch-judisches Nachleben* (Handbuch der Literaturwissenschaft). Wildpark-Potsdam: Akademische Verlagsgesellschaft Athenaion M.B.H., 1930.

—'Psalms, Book of', *IDB* III (1962), 942-958.

Hentschke, Richard *Die Stellung der vorexilischen Schriftpropheten zum Kultus* (BZAW). Berlin: Alfred Töpelmann, 1957.

Herbert, A.S. *The Book of the Prophet Isaiah* (CBC). Cambridge: The University Press, 1973, 2 vols.

—*Worship in Ancient Israel* (Ecumenical Studies in Worship 5). London: Lutterworth Press, 1959.

Hermisson, Hans-Jürgen *Sprache und Ritus im altisraelitischen Kult: Zur 'Spiritualisierung' Kultbegriffe im Alten Testament* (WMANT 19). Neukirchen-Vluyn: Neukirchener Verlag, 1965.

Hertzberg, H.W. 'Sind die Propheten Fürbitter?' *Tradition und Situation: Studien zur alttesta nentlichen Prophetie (Artur Weiser zum 70. Geburtstag).* Ed. Ernst Würthwein and Otto Kaiser. Göttingen: Vandenhoeck & Ruprecht, 1963: 63-74.

Heschel, Abraham J. *The Prophets.* New York: Harper & Row, 1962.

Hesse, Franz 'Wurzelt die prophetische Gerichtsrede im israelitischen Kult?' *ZAW* 65 (1953), 45-53.

Hirsch, Julius *Das Buch Jesaia.* Frankfurt: J. Kauffmann, 1911.

Holladay, William L. *The Root ŠÛBH in the Old Testament with Particular Reference to its Usages in Covenantal Contexts.* Leiden: E.J. Brill, 1958.

Hölscher, Gustav *Die Profeten: Untersuchungen zur Religionsgeschichte Israels.* Leipzig: J.C. Hinrichs'sche Buchhandlung, 1914.

Horst, Friedrich *Die Zwölf Kleinen Propheten, Nahum bis Maleachi* (Handbuch zum Alten Testament II, 14). Tübingen: J.C.B. Mohr (Paul Siebeck), 1938. (2nd ed. 1954.)

Humbert, Paul *Problèmes du Livre d'Habacuc* (Memoires de l'Université de Neuchâtel). Neuchâtel Secrétariat de l'Université, 1944.

Hyatt, James Philip *Commentary on Exodus* (New Century Bible). London: Oliphants, 1971.

Irwin, W.A. 'The Mythological Background of Habakkuk, Chapter 3', *JNES* 15 (1956), 47-50.

—'The Psalm of Habakkuk', *JNES* 1 (1942), 10-40.

Jastrow, Morris, Jr. *The Religion of Babylonia and Assyria* (Handbooks on the History of Religions). Boston: Ginn & Company, Publishers, 1898.

Jellicoe, Sidney 'The Prophets and the Cultus', *ExpT* 60 (1948-1949), 256-258.

Jepsen, Alfred *Nabi: Soziologische Studien zur alttestamentlichen L teratur und Religionsgeschichte*. München: C.H. Beck'sche Verlagsbuchhandlung, 1934.

Jeremias, Christian 'Zu Jes. XXXVIII 21f.', *VT* 21 (1971), 104-111.

Johnson, Aubrey R. *The Cultic Prophet and Israel's Psalmody*. Cardiff: University of Wales Press, 1979.

—*The Cultic Prophet in Ancient Israel*. Cardiff: University of Wales Press, 1944 (2nd ed. 1962).

—'The Prophet in Israelite Worship', *ExpT* 47 (1935-1936), 312-319.

—*Sacral Kingship in Ancient Israel*. Cardiff: University of Wales Press, 1955 (2nd ed. 1967).

Junker, Hubert *Prophet und Seher in Israel: Eine Untersuchung über die ältesten Erscheinungen des israelitischen Prophetentums, insbesondere den Prophetenvereine*. Trier: Paulinus-Verlag, 1927.

—'Unité, composition et genre littéraire des Psaumes IX et X', *RB* 60 (1935), 161-169.

Kaiser, Otto *Introduction to the Old Testament*. Trans. John Sturdy. Oxford: Basil Blackwell, 1975. [*Einleitung in das Alte Testament*, 2nd ed. Gütersloh: Gerd Mohn, 1970.]

—*Isaiah 13-39: A Commentary* (OTL). Trans. R.A. Wilson. London: SCM Press Ltd., 1974. [*Der Prophet Jesaja/Kap. 13–39* (Das Alte Testament Deutsch 18) Göttingen: Vandenhoeck & Ruprecht, 1973.]

Kapelrud, Arvid S. *Joel Studies* (Uppsala Universitets Årsskrift). Uppsala: A.-B. Lundequistska Bokhandeln, 1948.

Keller, Carl-A. 'Die Eigenart der Prophetie Habakuks', *ZAW* 85 (1973), 156-167.

Kilian, Rudolph 'Ps 22 und das priesterliche Heilsorakel', *BZ* n.f. 12 (1968), 172-185.

Kissane, Edward J. *The Book of Isaiah* I. Dublin: Browne and Nolan Limited, 1941.

Klatt, Werner *Hermann Gunkel. Zu seiner Theologie der Religionsgeschichte und zur Entstehung der formgeschichtlichen Methode* (FRLANT 100). Göttingen: Vandenhoeck & Ruprecht, 1969.

Klopfenstein, Martin A. *Scham und Schande nach dem Alten Testament: Eine begriffsgeschichtliche Untersuchung zu den hebräischen Wurzeln bôš, klm und hpr* (Abhandlungen zur Theologie des Alten und Neuen Testaments 62). Zürich: Theologischer Verlag, 1972.

Knuth, Hans Christian *Zur Auslegungsgeschichte von Psalm 6* (Beiträge zur Geschichte der Biblischen Exegese 11). Tübingen: J.C.B. Mohr (Paul Siebeck), 1971.

Köhler, Ludwig and Baumgartner, Walter, (ed.) *Lexicon in Veteris Testamenti Libros*. 2nd ed. Leiden: E.J. Brill, 1958.

Kraus, Hans-Joachim *Prophetie und Politik* (Theologische Existenz Heute n.f. 36). München: Chr. Kaiser Verlag, 1952.

—*Worship in Israel: A Cultic History of the Old Testament*. Trans. Geoffrey Buswell. Oxford: Basil Blackwell, 1966. [*Gottesdienst in Israel*, Munich: Chr. Kaiser Verlag, 1962.]

Küchler, Friedrich 'Das Priesterliche Orakel in Israel und Juda', *Abhandlungen zur semitischen Religionskunde und Sprachwissenschaft: Wolf Wilhelm Grafen von Baudissin zum 26. September 1917* (BZAW 33). Ed. Wilh. Frankenberg and Fried. Küchler. Giessen: Alfred Töpelmann, 1918, 285-301.

Kutsch, Ernst 'Heuschreckenplage und Tag Jahwes in Joel 1 und 2', *ThZ* 18 (1962), 81-94.

Laur, P. Elred 'Textstudie zum Canticum des Ezechias (Is 38,10-19)', *SMB* 28 (1907), 167-176.

Le Mat, L.A.F. *Textual Criticism and Exegesis of Psalm 36* (Studia theologica Rheno-Traiectina). Utrecht: Keminkt Zoon, 1957.

Leslie, Elmer A. *The Prophets Tell Their Own Story*. New York: Abingdon-Cokesbury Press, 1939.

Leveen, Jacob 'A Note on Psalm 10:17-18', *JBL* 67 (1948), 249-250.

—'Psalm X: A Reconstruction', *JTS* 45 (1944), 16-21.

Lindblom, Joh. 'Bemerkungen zu den Psalmen I', *ZAW* 59 (1942/43), 1-13.

—*Prophecy in Ancient Israel*. Oxford: Basil Blackwell, 1973.

—'Theophanies in Holy Places in Hebrew Religion', *HUCA* 32 (1961), 91-106.

Linder, Josef 'Textkritische und exegetische Studie zum Canticum Ezechiae (Is 38,9-20)', *ZKTh* 42 (1918), 46-73.

Lods, Adolphe *The Prophets and the Rise of Judaism* (The History of Civilization). Trans. S.H. Hooke. London: Routledge & Kegan Paul Ltd., 1937.

Löhr, Max 'Psalm 7 9 10', *ZAW* 36 (1916), 225-237.

McCarter, P. Kyle 'The River Ordeal in Israelite Literature', *HTR* 66 (1973), 403-412.

McKane, William *Proverbs: A New Approach* (OTL). London: SCM Press Ltd., 1970.

Margulis, Baruch 'The Psalm of Habakkuk: A Reconstruction and Interpretation', *ZAW* 82 (1970), 409-442.

Marti, Karl *Das Buch Jesaja* (Kurzer Hand-Commentar zum Alten Testament X). Tübingen: J.C.B. Mohr (Paul Siebeck), 1900.

Mauchline, John *Isaiah 1-39* (Torch Bible Commentaries). London: SCM Press Ltd., 1962.

May, Herbert Gordon 'Pattern and Myth in the Old Testament', *JR* 21 (1941), 285-299.

Meek, Theophile James *Hebrew Origins*. New York: Harper & Brothers, 1960.

Mettinger, Tryggve N.D. 'The Hebrew Verb System: A Survey of Recent Research', *Festschrift Hans Kosmala* (ASTI 9). Ed. Bengt Knutsson. Leiden: E.J. Brill, 1974: 64-84.

Michel, Diethelm *Tempora und Satzstellung in den Psalmen* (Abhandlungen zur Evangelischen Theologie 1). Bonn: H. Bouvier u. Co. Verlag, 1960.

Morgenstern, Julian 'Trial by Ordeal among the Semites and in Ancient Israel', *Hebrew Union College Jubilee Volume*. New York: KTAV Publishing House, Inc., 1925 (1968 reprint), 113-143.

Mowinckel, Sigmund 'Zum Psalm des Habakuk', *ThZ* 9 (1953), 1-23.

—*Psalmenstudien* I. '*Āwän* und die individuellen Klagepsalmen'. Amsterdam: Verlag P. Schippers N.V., 1966 reprint. Kristiania: Jacob Dybwad, 1921.

—*Psalmenstudien* II. 'Das Thronbesteigungsfest Jahwäs und der Ursprung der Eschatologie'. Amsterdam: Varlag P. Schippers N.V., 1966 reprint. Kristiania: Jacob Dybwad, 1922.

—*Psalmenstudien* III. 'Kultprophetie und Prophetische Psalmen'. Amsterdam: Verlag P. Schippers N.V., 1966 reprint. Kristiania: Jacob Dybwad, 1923.

—*Psalmenstudien* IV. 'Die Psalmdichter'. Amsterdam: Varlag P. Schippers N.V., 1966 reprint. Kristiania: Jacob Dybwad, 1924.

—*The Psalms in Israel's Worship*. Trans., D.R. Ap-Thomas. Oxford: Basil Blackwell, 1962. 2 vols.

—'"The Spirit" and the "Word" in the Pre-exilic Reforming Prophets', *JBL* 53 (1934), 199-227.

Muilenberg, James 'The Linguistic and Rhetorical Usages of the Particle כי in the Old Testament', *HUCA* 32 (1961), 135-160.

—'The "Office" of Prophet in Ancient Israel', *The Bible in Modern Scholarship*. Ed. James Philip Hyatt. London: Carey Kingsgate Press, 1965, 74-97.

Myers, Jacob M. 'Some Considerations Bearing on the Date of Joel', *ZAW* 74 (1962), 177-195.

Napier, B.D. 'Prophet, Prophetism', *IDB* III (1962), 896-919.

Nicolsky, N.M. 'Das Asylrecht in Israel', *ZAW* 48 (1930), 146-175.

—*Spuren magischer Formeln in den Psalmen* (BZAW 46). Trans., Georg Petzold. Giessen: Alfred Töpelmann, 1927.

Nielsen, Ed. 'The Righteous and the Wicked in Habaqquq', *StTh* 6 (1952), 54-78.

Noth, Martin 'Amt und Berufung im Alten Testament', *Gesammelte Studien zum Alten Testament* (Theologische Bücherei 6, 3rd ed.). München: Chr. Kaiser Verlag, 1966, 309-333.

—*Exodus: A Commentary* (OTL). Trans., J.S. Bowden. London: SCM Press Ltd., 1962. [*Das zweite Buch Mose, Exodus* (Das Alte Testament Deutsch 5). Göttingen: Vandenhoeck & Ruprecht, 1959.]

Nyberg, H.S. 'Hiskias Danklied Jes. 38,9-20', *Festschrift Hans Kosmala* (ASTI 9). Ed. Bengt Knutsson. Leiden: E.J. Brill, 1974, 85-97.

Oesterley, W.O.E. *Sacrifices in Ancient Israel: Their Origin, Purposes and Development*. London: Hodder and Stoughton, 1937.

Pedersen, Joh. *Israel: Its Life and Culture*. London: Oxford University Press, 1926 and 1940. 2 vols. and Copenhagen: Povl Branner (vol. 1) and Branner og Korch (vol. 2).

—'The Rôle Played by Inspired Persons Among the Israelites and the Arabs', *Studies in Old Testament Prophecy Presented to Theodore H. Robinson*. Ed. H.H. Rowley. Edinburgh: T. & T. Clark, 1957, 127-142.

Phillips, Anthony *Deuteronomy* (CBC). Cambridge: The University Press, 1973.

—'The Ecstatics' Father', *Words and Meanings: Essays Presented to David Winton Thomas*. Ed., Peter R. Ackroyd and Barnabas Lindars. Cambridge: The University Press, 1968, 183-194.

Plath, Margarete 'Joel 1:15-20', *ZAW* 47 (1929), 159-160.

Plöger, Otto 'Priester und Prophet', *ZAW* 63 (1951), 157-192.

Porteous, N.W. 'Prophet and Priest in Israel', *ExpT* 62 (1950-1951), 4-9.

Press, Richard 'Das Ordal im alten Israel', *ZAW* 51 (1933), 121-140, 227-255.

Pritchard, James B. (ed.) *Ancient Near Eastern Texts Relating to the Old Testament*. Princeton, N.J.: Princeton University Press, 1950.

Procksch, Otto *Jesaia* I (Kommentar zum Alten Testament IX). Leipzig: A. Deichertsche Verlagsbuchhandlung, 1930.

Quell, Gottfied 'Der Kultprophet', *ThLZ* 81 (1956), cols. 401-404.

von Rad, Gerhard *Deuteronomy: A Commentary* (OTL). Trans. Dorothea Barton. London: SCM Press Ltd., 1966. [*Das Fünfte Buch Mose: Deuteronomium* (Das Alte Testament Deutsch 8). Göttingen: Vandenhoeck & Ruprecht, 1964.]

—'Die falschen Propheten', *ZAW* 51 (1933), 109-120.

—*Old Testament Theology*. Trans. D.M.G. Stalker. London: Oliver and Boyd, 1962-1965, 2 vols. [*Theologie des Alten Testaments*. Munich: Chr. Kaiser Verlag, 1957-1960, 2 vols.]

—'"Righteousness" and "Life" in the Cultic Language of the Psalms', *The Problem of the Hexateuch and Other Essays*. Trans. E.W. Trueman Dicken. London: Oliver and Boyd, 1966, 243-266. [In *Festschrift für Alfred Berthelot*. Tübingen: 1950, 418-437 and *Gesammelte Studien zum Alten Testament*. Munich: Kaiser Verlag, 1958, 225-247.]

Rendtorff, Rolf 'נביא in the Old Testament', *TDNT* VI (1968), 796-812. [*TWNT* VI (1959), pp. 796-813.]

—'Priesterliche Kulttheologie und prophetische Kultpolemik', *ThLZ* 81 (1956), cols. 339-342.

Reventlow, Henning Graf 'Kultisches Recht im Alten Testament', *ZThK* 60 (1963), 267-304.

—'Prophetenamt und Mittleramt', *ZThK* 58 (1961), 269-284.

Ridderbos, Nic H. *Die Psalmen: Stilistische Verfahren und Aufbau mit besonderer Berücksichtigung von Ps 1-41* (BZAW 117). Trans. Karl E. Mittring. Berlin: Walter de Gruyter, 1972.

Ringgren, Helmer *The Faith of the Psalmists*. London: SCM Press Ltd., 1963.

—*Israelite Religion*. Trans. David Green. London: SPCK, 1966. [*Israelitische Religion*. Stuttgart: W. Kohlhammer Verlag, 1963.]

Ross, James F. 'Job 33:14-30: The Phenomenology of Lament', *JBL* 94 (1974), 38-46.

Rowley, H.H. 'The Nature of Old Testament Prophecy in the Light of Recent Study', *The Servant of the Lord and Other Essays on the Old Testament*. 2nd ed. Oxford: Basil Blackwell, 1952, 97-134.

—'Ritual and the Hebrew Prophets', *From Moses to Qumran: Studies in the Old Testament*. London: Lutterworth Press, 1963, 111-138.

—*Worship in Ancient Israel: Its Forms and Meaning* (Cadbury Lectures). London: SPCK, 1967.

Rudolph, Wilhelm *Joel-Amos-Obadja-Jona* (Kommentar zum Alten Testament XIII, 2). Gütersloh: Gerd Mohn, 1971.

—*Micha-Nahum-Habakuk-Zephanja* (Kommentar zum Alten Testament XIII, 3). Gütersloh: Gerd Mohn, 1975.

Schmidt, Hans *Das Gebet der Angeklagten im Alten Testament* (BZAW 49). Giessen: Alfred Töpelmann, 1928.

—'Das Gebet der Angeklagten im Alten Testament', *Old Testament Essays*. London: Charles Griffin and Company, Limited, 1927, 143-155.

—'Ein Psalm im Buche Habakuk', *ZAW* 62 (1950), 52-63.

—*Die Religiöse Lyrik im Alten Testament* (Religionsgeschichtliche Volksbücher II, 13). Tübingen: J.C.B. Mohr (Paul Siebeck), 1912.

Schoors, Antoon *I Am God Your Saviour: A Form-Critical Study of the Main Genres in Is. XL—LV* (SVT 24). Leiden: E.J. Brill, 1973.

Scott, R.B.Y. 'The Book of Isaiah' (Introduction and exegesis, chapters 1-39), *IB* V. New York: Abingdon Press, 1956.

—*The Relevance of the Prophets*. New York: The Macmillan Company, 1959.

Seebass, Horst 'בוש', *TDOT* II (1975), 50-60. [*TWAT* I (1972), 568-580.]

Sellin, Ernst *Das Zwölfprophetenbuch* (Kommentar zum Alten Testament XII, 3rd ed.). Leipzig: A. Deichertsche Verlagsbuchhandlung, 1930.

Seybold, Klaus *Das Gebet den Kranken im Alten Testament* (BWANT 99). Stuttgart: W. Kohlhammer, 1973.

Skinner, John *Prophecy and Religion: Studies in the Life of Jeremiah*. Cambridge: The University Press, 1930.

Smend, Rudolf 'Ueber das Ich der Psalmen', *ZAW* 8 (1888), 49-147.

Smith, W. Robertson *The Prophets of Israel and Their Place in History to the Close of the Eighth Century B.C.* London: Adam & Charles Black, 1895.

Snaith, Norman H. *The Distinctive Ideas of the Old Testament*. London: The Epworth Press, 1944 and Schocken Books, 1964.

Soggin, J. Alberto *Introduction to the Old Testament* (OTL). Trans. John Bowden. London: SCM Press Ltd., 1976.

—*Joshua: A Commentary* (OTL). Trans. R.A. Wilson. London: SCM Press, Ltd., 1972.

—'שוב', *THAT* II (1976), cols. 884-891.

Staerk, W. 'Zu Habakuk 1:5-11. Geschichte oder Mythos?' *ZAW* 51 (1933), 1-28.

Stephens, Ferris J. 'The Babylonian Dragon Myth in Habakkuk 3', *JBL* 43 (1924), 290-293.

Stoebe, Hans Joachim 'הסד', *THAT* I (1971), cols. 600-621.

—'טוב', *THAT* I (1971), cols. 652-664.

Stolz, F. 'בוש', *THAT* I (1971), cols. 269-272.

Strugnell, John 'A Note on Psalm CXXVI. 1', *JTS* n.s. 7 (1956), 239-243

Stummer, Friedrich *Sumerisch-Akkadische Parallelen zum Aufbau alttestamentlicher Psalmen* (Studien zur Geschichte und Kultur des Altertums II, 1). Paderborn: Ferdinand Schöningh, 1922.

Thomas, D. Winton, (ed.) *Documents from Old Testament Times*. London: Thomas Nelson and Sons and New York: Harper & Row, Publishers, 1958.

—'Some Observations on the Hebrew Root חסד', *Volume du congrès, Strasbourg 1956* (SVT 4), 1957, 8-16.

—*The Text of the Revised Psalter*. London: SPCK, 1963.

Thompson, John A. 'Joel's Locusts in the Light of Near Eastern Parallels', *JNES* 14 (1955), 52-55.

Torrey, C.C. 'The Archetype of Psalms 14 and 53', *JBL* 46 (1927), 186-192.

Treves, Marco 'The Date of Joel', *VT* 7 (1957), 149-156.

Tsevat, Matitiahu *A Study of the Language of the Biblical Psalms* (SBL Monograph series 9). Philadelphia: Society of Biblical Literature, 1955.

de Vaux, Roland *Ancient Israel: Its Life and Institutions*. Trans. John McHugh. London: Darton, Longman & Todd, 1961. [*Les Institutions de l'Ancien Testament*. Paris: Les Editions du Cerf, 1958-1960, 2 vols.]

Volz, Paul 'Die radikale Ablehnung der Kultreligion durch die alttestamentlichen Propheten', *ZST* 14 (1937), 63-85.

De Vries, S.J. 'Shame', *IDB* IV (1962), 305-306.

Vriezen, Th.C. *An Outline of Old Testament Theology*. Oxford: Basil Blackwell, 1958.

von Waldow, Eberhard *Der traditionsgeschichtliche Hintergrund der prophetischen Gerichtsreden* (BZAW 85). Berlin: Alfred Töpelmann, 1963.

Walker, H.H. and Lund, N.W. 'The Literary Structure of the Book of Habakkuk', *JBL* 53 (1934), 355-370.

Ward, William Hayes *A Critical and Exegetical Commentary on Habakkuk* (International Critical Commentary). Edinburgh: T. & T. Clark, 1912.

Watters, William R. *Formula Criticism and the Poetry of the Old Testament* (BZAW 138). Berlin: Walter de Gruyter, 1976.

Watts, John D.W. *The Books of Joel, Obadiah, Jonah, Nahum, Habakkuk and Zephaniah* (CBC). Cambridge: The University Press, 1975.

Weinfeld, Moshe 'Ancient Near Eastern Patterns in Prophetic Literature', *VT* 27 (1977), 178-195.

Weiser, Artur *The Old Testament: Its Formation and Development*. New York: Association Press, 1961. [*Einleitung in das Alten Testament*, 4th ed. Göttingen: Vandenhoeck & Ruprecht, 1957.]

Welch, Adam C. *Prophet and Priest in Old Israel*. London: SCM Press Ltd., 1936.

Westermann, Claus *Basic Forms of Prophetic Speech*. Trans. Hugh Clayton White. London: Lutterworth Press, 1967. [*Grundformen Prophetischer Rede*. Munich: Chr. Kaiser Verlag.]

—*The Praise of God in the Psalms*. Trans. Keith R. Crim. London: Epworth Press, 1961. [*Das Loben Gottes in den Psalmen*, Göttingen: Vandenhoeck & Ruprecht, 1961.]

—'The Role of the Lament in the Theology of the Old Testament'. Trans. Richard N. Soulen. *Interpretation* 28 (1974), 20-38.

—'Struktur und Geschichte der Klage im Alten Testament', *ZAW* 66 (1954), 44-80.

Wevers, John Wm. 'A Study in the Form Criticism of Individual Complaint Psalms', *VT* 6 (1956), 80-96.

Whitehouse, Owen C. *Isaiah* I (The Century Bible). London: Caxton Publishing Company, n.d.

Widengren, Geo *The Accadian and Hebrew Psalms of Lamentation as Religious Documents: A Comparative Study*. Stockholm: Bokförlags Aktiebolaget Thule, 1937.

Wolff, Hans Walter *Joel and Amos: A Commentary on the Books of the Prophets Joel and Amos* (Hermeneia). Trans. Waldemar Janzen, S. Dean McBride, Jr., and Charles A. Muenchow. Ed. S. Dean McBride, Jr. Philadelphia: Fortress Press, 1977. [*Dodekapropheton 2. Joel und Amos*, 2nd ed. (BKAT XIV/2) Neukirchner-Vluyn: Neukirchner Verlag, 1975.]

Würthwein, Ernst 'Kultpolemic oder Kultbescheid? Beobachtungen zu dem Thema "Prophetie und Kult"', *Tradition und Situation: Studien zur alttestamentlichen Prophetie (Artur Weiser zum 70. Geburtstag)*. Ed. Ernst Würthwein and Otto Kaiser. Göttingen: Vandenhoeck & Ruprecht, 1963, 115-131.

—'Der Ursprung der prophetischen Gerichtsrede', *ZThK* 49 (1952), 1-16.

Zimmerli, Walther חסר', *TDNT* IX (1974), 381-387. [*TWNT* IX, 1973, 372-377.]

Zimmern, Heinrich *Babylonische Hymnen und Gebete* (Der alte Orient VIII, 3). Leipzig: J.C. Hinrichs'sche Buchhandlung, 1905.

Zobel, Hans-Jürgen 'Das Gebet um Abwendung der Not und seine Erhörung in den Klageliedern des Alten Testaments und in der Inschrift des Königs Zakir von Hamath', *VT* 21 (1971), 91-99.

INDEXES

INDEX OF BIBLICAL REFERENCES

INDEX OF SUBJECTS

INDEX OF AUTHORS